FLORIDA BUCKET LIST

Set Off on **120 Epic Adventures** and Discover Incredible Destinations to Live Out Your Dreams While Creating Unforgettable Memories that Will Last a Lifetime.

(Online Digital MAP included - access it through the link provided in the MAP Chapter of this book)

BeCrePress Travel

FLORIDA BUCKET LIST

table of contents

FLORIDA BUCKET LIST

TABLE OF CONTENTS

FLORIDA BUCKET LIST

FLORIDA BUCKET LIST

FLORIDA BUCKET LIST

FLORIDA BUCKET LIST

INTRODUCTION

Welcome to *Florida Bucket List: Set Off on 120 Epic Adventures and Discover Incredible Destinations to Live Out Your Dreams*—your ultimate guide to exploring the Sunshine State like never before! Whether you're a local Floridian ready to rediscover your home state or a first-time visitor looking for the perfect blend of adventure, relaxation, and culture, this book is your key to experiencing Florida's most beautiful and unforgettable destinations.

Picture yourself basking in the warm glow of a sunset over the Gulf of Mexico, your toes sinking into sugar-white sand. Imagine snorkeling through the crystalline waters of a coral reef, encountering vibrant marine life up close. Or perhaps you envision yourself walking through a historic fort, where centuries-old walls whisper tales of the past. Florida offers all this and more, from its pristine beaches to its lush parks, cultural landmarks, and thrilling theme parks.

This book is designed to not only take you to Florida's most attractive destinations but also to ignite your sense of adventure and inspire unforgettable memories. With 120 carefully curated spots, you'll discover everything from hidden gems tucked away in nature to world-famous attractions that define Florida's allure. Whether you're a beach lover, a history buff, a nature enthusiast, or a theme park thrill-seeker, you'll find your perfect adventure within these pages.

Each destination is laid out with all the essential information to make your journey effortless and enjoyable. You won't have to scramble for details or search endlessly for directions. Here's what you can expect for every adventure:

- **A description of the destination**: Every place comes with an engaging and vivid description that paints a picture in your mind. Whether it's the serenity of a secluded beach or the excitement of a bustling boardwalk, we'll help you feel like you're already there.

- The address: Clear and precise, so you know exactly where to go and avoid any confusion when you're on the road.

- **The nearest city**: Each destination includes the nearest city, giving you a point of reference to better understand where you're headed in relation to Florida's larger urban centers.

- **GPS coordinates:** We provide the exact coordinates so you can plug them into your GPS and let technology lead the way. No guesswork, no missed turns—just smooth, stress-free travel.

- **The best time to visit**: Want to know when the crowds are lightest, the weather is perfect, or when a destination is at its most magical? We've got you covered with the best time to visit each spot, ensuring your experience is top-notch.

- **Tolls and access fees**: Traveling is more enjoyable when you're prepared. We've included all the details about any tolls, parking fees, or entry costs so there are no surprises along the way.

- **Did you know?**: Every destination comes with a fascinating piece of trivia or history, something you may not have known before but will definitely appreciate. From quirky facts to historical tidbits, these nuggets will enrich your visit and make your adventures even more memorable.

- **Website:** Stay up to date with each destination by checking the official websites we've included. Whether it's for planning your visit or checking for any last-minute changes, these links will keep you informed.

And as a special bonus, we've included an interactive **State Map** with all the destinations from this guide already loaded. Say goodbye to the hassle of manually plotting your trip! This digital map ensures you can easily locate and plan your visits without wasting time or risking mistakes. Whether you're using it to create a well-planned road trip or exploring a particular region in depth, the map makes it easy to visualize your adventure and stay organized.

This guide isn't just about seeing Florida; it's about experiencing it. It's about feeling the wind on your face as you sail through the Keys, hearing the distant roar of waves as you walk along a tranquil beach, tasting the fresh seafood caught just that morning, and soaking in the magic of a sunset that you'll remember for the rest of your life. Every page of this book is designed to inspire you, spark your curiosity, and help you create stories you'll be sharing for years to come.

So, are you ready to embark on the adventure of a lifetime? Whether you're looking for the thrill of exploring underwater caves, the peace of a secluded nature preserve, or the excitement of Florida's famous theme parks, this guide has it all. Adventure, beauty, and wonder await you in every corner of this incredible state—and now, with Florida Bucket List in hand, you have everything you need to explore them.

So grab your map, charge your camera, and let's set off on 120 epic adventures that will make your dreams come to life and create memories that will last a lifetime! Whether you're looking for that perfect getaway, a family adventure, or a solo retreat, this guide will take you to the most awe-inspiring spots Florida has to offer. Ready to explore? Your unforgettable journey starts now!

ABOUT FLORIDA

To access the <u>Digital Map</u>, please refer to the 'Map Chapter' in this book

Landscape of Florida

Florida's landscape is a kaleidoscope of natural wonders, where the scenery shifts from emerald-green swamps to sun-kissed beaches and shimmering waterways, each more captivating than the last. This is a land where nature's artistry meets a vibrant palette of ecosystems that stretch across the peninsula, forming a unique environment that enchants visitors from all over the world.

Imagine standing on the edge of a pristine white-sand beach, where the gentle waves of the Atlantic Ocean or the Gulf of Mexico lap at your feet, or trekking through lush forests where towering pines, palms, and centuries-old oaks provide shade beneath the warm Floridian sun.

Florida's foundation is built on a bedrock of limestone, shaped over millennia by the forces of nature. Beneath the surface lies a vast network of freshwater aquifers, which nourish the land and create the magical springs that dot the region.

The state is home to some of the most expansive wetlands in the world, including the iconic Everglades, where mangroves and sawgrass marshes stretch as far as the eye can see, creating a delicate balance between land and water. This unique ecosystem, often called the "River of Grass," teems with life, from alligators to manatees and a breathtaking array of bird species.

Further north, the rolling hills of central Florida, though modest, contrast with the flat, open expanses of the south. These ridges provide a scenic backdrop, where citrus groves fill the air with the sweet scent of oranges. Whether it's the serenity of the swamplands, the grandeur of the forests, or the allure of the sparkling waters, Florida's diverse landscape paints a vivid picture that invites exploration and adventure at every turn. Each corner of this vibrant state offers a different view of nature's beauty, where every horizon holds the promise of discovery.

Flora and Fauna of Florida

Florida's flora and fauna weave together a vibrant tapestry of life, a stunning reminder of nature's diversity and resilience. With its unique blend of tropical, subtropical, and temperate climates, the state nurtures a lush array of plant life that blankets the landscape with verdant beauty. Towering palm trees sway in the coastal breezes, while majestic live oaks, draped in Spanish moss, create dreamy canopies across the interior.

Cypress swamps, their knobby roots rising from the waters like ancient sculptures, thrive in the wetlands, and the sweet fragrance of orange blossoms fills the air in the northern and central parts of the state.

Mangroves, with their tangled roots gripping the shoreline, serve as both protectors and nurseries for marine life along Florida's coastlines.

The fauna of Florida is equally enchanting, offering encounters with wildlife that feel almost magical. Imagine spotting a manatee lazily drifting through crystal-clear springs or witnessing the graceful glide of a bottlenose dolphin off the coast. The Everglades are home to the iconic American alligator, a symbol of Florida's wild heart, while further south, the elusive Florida panther prowls in the shadows of cypress forests.

Birdwatchers will be captivated by the vibrant splashes of color provided by flamingos, roseate spoonbills, and the majestic bald eagle soaring overhead.

But it's not just the larger species that capture the imagination. Florida's subtropical climate supports an astonishing variety of smaller creatures, from butterflies fluttering through wildflower meadows to the chorus of frogs serenading at dusk. The state's coral reefs, teeming with life, are a breathtaking underwater wonderland, home to colorful fish, sea turtles, and a kaleidoscope of marine species.

In Florida, nature's beauty is everywhere—on land, in the sky, and beneath the waters—inviting visitors to immerse themselves in its wonder and splendor.

Climate of Florida

Florida's climate is a dream for sun-seekers, offering warmth and sunshine nearly year-round, creating an irresistible allure for travelers. Picture stepping off the plane and being greeted by a balmy breeze, the air kissed by tropical warmth. The Sunshine State earns its name, with an average of 230 days of sunshine per year, casting a golden glow over its beaches, forests, and cities alike.

Florida's climate is a delightful blend of tropical and subtropical, meaning that the southern tip of the state, including the Keys, enjoys a true tropical climate, while the northern and central regions experience subtropical weather.

Summer days here are long and warm, with temperatures often climbing into the high 80s and 90s (30-35°C), but the sea breeze, ever-present, keeps the heat from overwhelming.

Picture yourself enjoying a cool drink on a breezy boardwalk as the sun begins to set over the Gulf of Mexico, painting the sky in shades of pink and orange.

Summers also bring the thrill of afternoon thunderstorms—short bursts of rain that refresh the air and make way for vibrant sunsets.

These dramatic downpours, complete with lightning dancing across the sky, are part of Florida's natural charm.

Winters in Florida are a warm refuge from the chill gripping other parts of the country. From December to February, the weather remains mild, with temperatures ranging from the mid-60s to low 70s (18-24°C), making it a perfect destination for those escaping the cold. Picture yourself strolling along the coast, enjoying the gentle warmth of the winter sun as it glistens off the water.

Florida's tropical storms and hurricanes, while a natural part of life in the region, also contribute to the dramatic beauty of its skies and the lush, verdant landscape that thrives under the state's abundant rainfall.

History of Florida

Florida's history is as rich and diverse as the vibrant landscapes that define its geography. A land of natural beauty and cultural convergence, its story is woven with tales of exploration, conquest, and transformation—each chapter contributing to the state's dynamic identity today.

Long before Florida became a prized destination for travelers, it was home to indigenous peoples who lived off its rich natural resources. The first inhabitants arrived thousands of years ago, leaving traces of their existence through artifacts, mounds, and ancient settlements. Among these early civilizations were the Calusa, Timucua, and Apalachee, who thrived in various regions of the peninsula. Their cultures were deeply connected to the land and sea, where they fished, hunted, and developed complex societies.

The European encounter with Florida began in 1513, when Spanish explorer Juan Ponce de León arrived on its eastern shores. Legend holds that he was searching for the fabled Fountain of Youth, but what he found instead was a landscape so stunning and fertile that he named it "La Florida," meaning "Land of Flowers." Ponce de León's discovery marked the beginning of European interest in the region, setting the stage for centuries of colonial conflict.

Spain laid claim to Florida, establishing St. Augustine in 1565, which today stands as the oldest continuously inhabited European settlement in the United States. For more than two centuries, the Spanish controlled Florida, building missions, forts, and a thriving colonial economy. However, the state's strategic location meant it was a highly coveted prize. French, British, and Spanish forces clashed repeatedly over the territory, each seeking to dominate its trade routes and resources.

By the mid-18th century, Florida found itself under British rule following the Treaty of Paris in 1763. The British divided Florida into East and West colonies, hoping to develop the land further. However, the British influence was short-lived, and after the American Revolution, Florida returned to Spanish control under the Second Spanish Period. It wasn't until 1821, after years of diplomatic negotiation, that Florida became a U.S. territory through the Adams-Onís Treaty, finally joining the growing nation's fold.

As a U.S. territory, Florida's growth accelerated, though not without turmoil. The state became a hotspot for conflict, as Seminole Wars erupted between the U.S. government and the Seminole people, who fiercely resisted relocation efforts. These wars were among the most expensive and longest conflicts involving Native Americans in U.S. history. Despite the hardships, the Seminoles, who had found refuge in the Everglades, remained a resilient part of Florida's cultural fabric.

Florida's status as a U.S. state came in 1845, and it quickly became a battleground during the Civil War. Though a member of the Confederacy, much of Florida remained a contested frontier throughout the conflict, serving as a critical supplier of cattle, salt, and other resources for the Southern war effort. The state's coastline, with its strategic ports, attracted the Union's blockade forces, creating a tense and dynamic warfront.

In the post-Civil War era, Florida began its transformation into the paradise that visitors know today. The late 19th century brought the arrival of visionary entrepreneurs like Henry Flagler and Henry Plant, who extended railroad lines into Florida's wilderness, unlocking the state's vast potential for tourism and agriculture. Their efforts turned once-remote areas into bustling resorts and towns, drawing wealthy Northerners to escape the bitter winters and enjoy Florida's warm, sunny climate.

As the state entered the 20th century, it experienced rapid development. The construction of the Overseas Railroad in the early 1900s linked the Florida Keys to the mainland, creating new opportunities for exploration and tourism. Agriculture boomed, particularly the citrus industry, with Florida's oranges becoming synonymous with the state itself. Land speculation and real estate booms shaped cities like Miami and Tampa, transforming them into modern hubs of commerce and leisure.

Florida's history took another leap in the mid-20th century with the arrival of Walt Disney World, forever changing the state's cultural and economic landscape. When the Magic Kingdom opened its gates in 1971, it solidified Florida's place as a global tourism mecca, attracting millions of visitors annually. Disney's magical vision inspired an explosion of development around Orlando, turning central Florida into a theme park wonderland, with destinations like Universal Studios and SeaWorld following suit.

Beyond its theme parks and sun-soaked beaches, Florida has also played a pivotal role in the nation's space exploration efforts. The state's Kennedy Space Center, located on the eastern coast, has been the launch site for countless historic missions, including the Apollo moon landings and Space Shuttle launches. This connection to the cosmos has given Florida a unique place in American history, symbolizing innovation and the pursuit of knowledge.

Florida's more recent history has been marked by its rapid population growth and continued attraction as a destination for retirees, families, and adventurers. Its blend of diverse cultures—shaped by waves of

Cuban, Caribbean, and Latin American immigration—has created a rich, vibrant tapestry of communities. From the art deco streets of Miami Beach to the historic charm of St. Augustine, Florida's cities are alive with cultural heritage and creativity.

The state's natural beauty has remained at the heart of its allure, even as it has grown and evolved. Florida is a place where history and nature intertwine, from the wild expanses of the Everglades to the preserved forts and settlements that dot the coastline. It is a place where centuries-old stories are still whispered in the winds that blow through the ancient live oaks, and where the dreams of explorers and pioneers continue to shape the future.

In its past lies the foundation for its future, and in Florida's story, you'll find tales of resilience, transformation, and endless reinvention. Whether you are wandering through the cobblestone streets of St. Augustine or marveling at the rocket launches along the Space Coast, you are stepping into a rich historical narrative that makes Florida far more than just a vacation destination—it's a place where history comes alive, and the possibilities are as boundless as the horizon.

How to Use this Guide

Welcome to your comprehensive guide to exploring Minnesota! This chapter is dedicated to helping you understand how to effectively use this guide and the interactive map to enhance your travel experience. Let's dive into the simple steps to navigate the book and utilize the digital tools provided, ensuring you have the best adventure possible.

Understanding the Guide's Structure

The guide features 120 of the best destinations across the beautiful state of Minnesota, thoughtfully compiled to inspire and facilitate your explorations. These destinations are divided into areas and listed alphabetically. This organization aims to simplify your search process, making it quick and intuitive to locate each destination in the book.

Using the Alphabetical Listings

Since the destination areas are arranged alphabetically, you can easily flip through the guide to find a specific place or browse areas that catch your interest. Each destination entry in the book includes essential information such as:

- A vivid description of the destination.

- The complete address and the nearest major city, giving you a quick geographical context.

- GPS coordinates for precise navigation.

- The best times to visit, helping you plan your trip according to seasonal attractions and weather.

- Details on tolls or access fees, preparing you for any costs associated with your visit.

- Fun trivia to enhance your knowledge and appreciation of each location.

- A link to the official website for up-to-date information.

To further enhance your experience and save time, you can scan these website links using apps like Google Lens to open them directly without the need to type them into a browser. This seamless integration allows for quicker access to the latest information and resources about each destination.

Navigating with the Interactive State Map

Your guide comes equipped with an innovative tool—an interactive map of Minnesota that integrates seamlessly with Google Maps. This digital map is pre-loaded with all 120 destinations, offering an effortless way to visualize and plan your journey across the state.

How to Use the Map:

- **Open the Interactive Map**: Start by accessing the digital map through the link provided in your guide. You can open it on any device that supports Google Maps, such as a smartphone, tablet, or computer.

- **Choose Your Starting Point:** Decide where you will begin your adventure. You might start from your current location or another specific point in Minnesota.

- **Explore Nearby Destinations:** With the map open, zoom in and out to view the destinations near your starting point. Click on any marker to see a brief description and access quick links for navigation and more details.

- **Plan Your Itinerary:** Based on the destinations close to your chosen start, you can create a personalized itinerary. You can select multiple locations to visit in a day or plan a more extended road trip through various regions.

Combining the Book and Map for Best Results

To get the most out of your adventures:

- <u>Cross-Reference</u>: Use the interactive map to spot destinations you are interested in and then refer back to the guidebook for detailed information and insights.

- <u>Plan Sequentially:</u> As you plan your route on the map, use the alphabetical listing in the book to easily gather information on each destination and organize your visits efficiently.

- <u>Stay Updated:</u> Regularly check the provided website links for any changes in operation hours, fees, or special events at the destinations.

By following these guidelines and utilizing both the guidebook and the interactive map, you will be well-equipped to explore Minnesota's diverse landscapes and attractions.

Whether you are seeking solitude in nature, adventure in the outdoors, or cultural experiences in urban settings, this guide will serve as your reliable companion, ensuring every adventure is memorable and every discovery is enriching. Happy travels!

AMELIA ISLAND

Fort Clinch State Park

Find your sense of adventure at Fort Clinch State Park, a historical gem situated on Amelia Island. This park, with its well-preserved 19th-century fort, offers a captivating blend of history and natural beauty. Located in Fernandina Beach, Fort Clinch invites visitors to step back in time and explore the past while enjoying the present. With activities such as hiking, fishing, wildlife watching, and guided tours, this park is a hub for both recreation and education. One of the park's unique features is the opportunity to camp within sight of the historic fort, making for an unforgettable experience.

Location: 2601 Atlantic Ave, Fernandina Beach, Amelia Island, FL 32034-2203

Closest City or Town: Fernandina Beach, Florida

How to Get There: Take I-95 to Exit 373 for FL-200/FL-A1A East towards Fernandina Beach; continue on FL-200/FL-A1A East, follow signs for the park.

GPS Coordinates: 30.7013867° N, 81.4537293° W

Best Time to Visit: Spring and Fall for mild weather

Pass/Permit/Fees: Entrance fee of $6 per vehicle

Did You Know? Fort Clinch was never attacked during the Civil War but remained a valuable base of operations for Union forces.

Website: http://www.floridastateparks.org/park/Fort-Clinch

BAY LAKE

Disney's Hollywood Studios

Step into the magic at Disney's Hollywood Studios, a vibrant theme park located in Bay Lake. This destination captures the glamour of Hollywood's Golden Age while offering numerous attractions inspired by blockbuster movies and TV shows. From the thrilling Tower of Terror to the whimsical Toy Story Land, there's something to excite everyone. Situated within the Walt Disney World Resort, Disney's Hollywood Studios provides endless fun and entertainment. Visitors can also savor character dining experiences, capture photos with beloved Disney characters, and enjoy nightly spectaculars. The park's unique blend of classic Hollywood and imaginative worlds sets the stage for countless adventures.

Location: 351 South Studio Drive Streets of America, Bay Lake, FL 32830

Closest City or Town: Orlando, Florida

How to Get There: Accessible via I-4 or World Drive; follow signs to Disney's Hollywood Studios within Walt Disney World Resort.

GPS Coordinates: 28.3580628° N, 81.5590975° W

Best Time to Visit: Weekdays during the off-season months (January, February, September)

Pass/Permit/Fees: Admission requires a Walt Disney World ticket; prices vary.

Did You Know? The park features an exact replica of the Grauman's Chinese Theatre that houses the Great Movie Ride.

Website: http://disneyworld.disney.go.com/destinations/hollywood-studios/?CMP=OKC-wdw_TA_119A

Magic Kingdom Park

Embark on a fantastical journey at the Magic Kingdom Park, the iconic heart of the Walt Disney World Resort in Bay Lake. Famous for Cinderella Castle, this park brings beloved fairy tales to life through enchanting lands such as Fantasyland, Adventureland, and Tomorrowland. Wander along Main Street, U.S.A., relive classic rides, and meet your favorite Disney characters. The park's parades and spectacular fireworks shows are a must-see, bringing a magical end to every day. Magic Kingdom is the ultimate destination for creating lifelong memories, where dreams come true and the magic never ends.

Location: 1180 Seven Seas Dr Walt Disney World, Bay Lake, FL 32836

Closest City or Town: Orlando, Florida

How to Get There: Follow signs to Magic Kingdom from I-4 or World Drive within Walt Disney World; park using the Transportation and Ticket Center.

GPS Coordinates: 28.4048775° N, 81.5803605° W

Best Time to Visit: Weekdays during early spring or late fall

Pass/Permit/Fees: Requires a Walt Disney World ticket; prices vary.

Did You Know? The Uptown Jewelers shop on Main Street, U.S.A., mirrors the design of the City Hall in Los Angeles.

Website: http://disneyworld.disney.go.com/destinations/magic-kingdom/?CMP=OKC-wdw_TA_189/)

BIG PINE KEY

Bahia Honda State Park

Discover pristine beauty at Bahia Honda State Park, a tropical paradise nestled on Big Pine Key. Famed for its crystal-clear turquoise waters and sandy beaches, this park offers some of the best snorkeling and beachcombing in Florida. Located at Mile Marker 37 along the Overseas Highway, Bahia Honda invites visitors to swim, kayak, and explore underwater adventures. Nature trails provide an opportunity to observe native wildlife and breathtaking vistas. One of the park's unique attractions is the historic Old Bahia Honda Bridge, offering panoramic views of the bay. Bahia Honda's natural charm makes it a must-visit destination in the Keys.

Location: 36850 Overseas Hwy, Big Pine Key, FL 33043-3517

Closest City or Town: Marathon, Florida

How to Get There: Drive south on US-1 from Miami, passing through the Florida Keys until reaching Mile Marker 37.

GPS Coordinates: 24.6639252° N, 81.2590310° W

Best Time to Visit: Late fall to early spring for optimal weather

Pass/Permit/Fees: $8 per vehicle, $4.50 single occupant

Did You Know? The park's name, Bahia Honda, means Deep Bay in Spanish, referring to the natural deep waters found near the shore.

Website: https://www.floridastateparks.org/BahiaHonda

BOCA RATON

Gumbo Limbo Nature Center

Uncover the wonders of marine life and coastal ecosystems at Gumbo Limbo Nature Center in Boca Raton. Nestled on Ocean Boulevard, this center offers an immersive experience into the area's natural environment. Visitors can explore butterfly gardens, sandy beach trails, and interactive marine exhibits. Located within the Red Reef Park, Gumbo Limbo is also home to rehabilitative programs for injured sea turtles. The unique outdoor aquariums and boardwalk trail through a coastal hammock provide a fascinating glimpse into the interactions of plant and animal life. This nature center serves as a beacon for environmental education and wildlife conservation.

Location: 1801 N Ocean Blvd, Boca Raton, FL 33432-1946

Closest City or Town: Boca Raton, Florida

How to Get There: From I-95, take exit 48A to merge onto FL-794 E/W. Yamato Rd. Continue on FL-794 E, then turn right onto US-1 S/N Federal Hwy, and left onto NE Spanish River Blvd. Turn right onto N Ocean Blvd.

GPS Coordinates: 26.3661960° N, 80.0702040° W

Best Time to Visit: Late fall through spring

Pass/Permit/Fees: Free admission; donations are welcomed.

Did You Know? The name Gumbo Limbo is derived from a native tree in the area that has distinct, peeling red bark.

Website: http://myboca.us/gumbolimbo

CLEARWATER

Pier 60

Find your sense of excitement at Pier 60, the heart of Clearwater Beach. Located in Clearwater, Florida, this iconic pier stretches into the Gulf of Mexico, offering stunning sunset views that will leave you breathless. Stroll along the pier, try your hand at fishing, or simply relax and enjoy the live entertainment and local crafts showcased at the nightly Sunsets at Pier 60 festival. You'll find that Pier 60 is more than just a pier—it's a vibrant gathering place that epitomizes the lively spirit of Clearwater Beach.

Location: 7 Causeway Blvd, Clearwater, FL 33767-2003

Closest City or Town: Clearwater, Florida

How to Get There: From US-19, take the FL-60 W exit towards Clearwater Beach. Follow FL-60 W (Causeway Blvd) until you reach the roundabout at Clearwater Beach. Pier 60 will be directly ahead.

GPS Coordinates: 27.9776638° N, 82.8287749° W

Best Time to Visit: Visit during the late afternoon to enjoy the Sunsets at Pier 60 festival.

Pass/Permit/Fees: Admission to the pier area is free; fishing poles are available for rent on-site for various fees.

Did You Know? Pier 60 is renowned for its daily Sunset Celebration, featuring numerous local artisans, performers, and musicians.

Website: https://www.visitstpeteclearwater.com/profile/pier-60-clearwater-beach/1570

COCOA BEACH

Cocoa Beach

Ride the perfect wave at Cocoa Beach, the East Coast surfing capital. Nestled along Florida's Space Coast, Cocoa Beach offers endless sun, sand, and surf. Known for its family-friendly atmosphere and historic pier, it's a paradise for beachgoers and water sports enthusiasts alike. Enjoy a paddleboarding adventure, take a surf lesson, or visit the iconic Ron Jon Surf Shop. Whether you're basking in the sun or exploring the surf, Cocoa Beach promises a lively and laid-back coastal experience.

Location: 1600 Minutemen Causeway, Cocoa Beach, FL 32932

Closest City or Town: Cocoa Beach, Florida

How to Get There: From I-95, take exit 201 to merge onto FL-520 E/W King St toward Cocoa Beach. Continue on FL-520 E until you reach the beachside.

GPS Coordinates: 28.3176675° N, 80.6328395° W

Best Time to Visit: Spring and summer months offer ideal beach weather.

Pass/Permit/Fees: Beach access is free; parking fees may apply depending on the lot.

Did You Know? Cocoa Beach is home to the world-famous Ron Jon Surf Shop, the largest of its kind.

Website: https://www.cityofcocoabeach.com/

DAYTONA BEACH

Beach at Daytona Beach

Soak up the sun at Daytona Beach, The World's Most Famous Beach. Located along Florida's Atlantic coast, Daytona Beach is synonymous with wide, sandy shores, thrilling motorsports, and vibrant nightlife. Dive into beach volleyball, cast a line from the pier, or drive along the sandy stretches of the beach itself—a rare experience in today's world. With its bustling Boardwalk and arcade attractions, Daytona Beach is an exuberant blend of sun-soaked relaxation and high-energy fun.

Location: 301 S. Ridgewood Avenue, Daytona Beach, FL 32114

Closest City or Town: Daytona Beach, Florida

How to Get There: From I-95, take exit 261 for US-92 E toward Daytona Beach. Follow US-92 E/W International Speedway Blvd until you reach S. Ridgewood Avenue, then head east to the beach.

GPS Coordinates: 29.2108147° N, 81.0228331° W

Best Time to Visit: Spring and summer months are ideal for beach activities.

Pass/Permit/Fees: Beach access is free, but parking fees may apply in certain areas.

Did You Know? The hard-packed sands of Daytona Beach allow vehicles to drive directly on the beach, a tradition that dates back to the early 20th century.

Website: https://www.daytonabeach.com/things-to-do/beaches/

Daytona International Speedway

Feel the adrenaline rush at Daytona International Speedway, the epicenter of American motorsports. Situated in Daytona Beach, Florida, this world-renowned racetrack hosts the iconic Daytona 500, attracting motorsports fans from around the globe. Explore the high-banked turns, engage in interactive NASCAR exhibits, and experience the thrill of a racing simulator. With behind-the-scenes tours and unforgettable race day experiences, the Speedway offers a high-octane adventure for everyone.

Location: 1801 W International Speedway Blvd, Daytona Beach, FL 32114-1215

Closest City or Town: Daytona Beach, Florida

How to Get There: From I-95, take exit 261 for US-92 E toward Daytona Beach. Follow US-92 E/W International Speedway Blvd; the speedway will be on your left.

GPS Coordinates: 29.1919290° N, 81.0678660° W

Best Time to Visit: February during the Daytona 500, or anytime there's a race event.

Pass/Permit/Fees: Fees vary depending on the event and tour options; check the website for details.

Did You Know? The Daytona International Speedway can accommodate over 100,000 spectators, making it one of the largest single spectator venues in the world.

Website:
http://www.daytonainternationalspeedway.com/?homepage=true

DeLand

Stetson Mansion

Step back in time at the opulent Stetson Mansion, a testament to Gilded Age grandeur. Located in DeLand, Florida, this Victorian masterpiece was built by famed hat maker John B. Stetson in 1886. Wander through exquisitely restored rooms, marvel at the intricate parquet floors, and be enchanted by the opulent holiday displays during Christmas. The Mansion's stunning blend of Gothic, Tudor, and Moorish styles make it a unique historical treasure.

Location: 1031 Camphor Ln, DeLand, FL 32720-5003

Closest City or Town: DeLand, Florida

How to Get There: From I-4, take exit 118A-B for FL-44 W toward DeLand Historic District. Continue on FL-44 W, then turn right onto S. Blue Lake Ave, then left on Camphor Ln.

GPS Coordinates: 29.0232412° N, 81.3230028° W

Best Time to Visit: Year-round, with special holiday tours in December.

Pass/Permit/Fees: Entrance fees vary, with special discounts available online.

Did You Know? The Stetson Mansion incorporates over 10,000 panes of antique glass in its windows, each individually hand-cut and imported from Germany.

Website: http://www.stetsonmansion.com/

DELRAY BEACH

Morikami Museum & Japanese Gardens

Embark on a journey of tranquility at Morikami Museum & Japanese Gardens, an enchanting oasis tucked away in Delray Beach, Florida. Immerse yourself in the serene beauty of traditional Japanese landscaping, cultural exhibits, and zen-inspired architecture. Located in Morikami Park, the museum offers a unique glimpse into Japanese culture, inspired by the Yamato Colony settlers who arrived in Florida in the early 20th century.

Visitors can meander through six distinct gardens, inspired by famous garden styles throughout Japanese history, and participate in vibrant cultural festivals or tea ceremonies. Taste authentic Japanese cuisine at the on-site café, all while soaking in the peaceful ambiance.

Location: 4000 Morikami Park Rd, Delray Beach, FL 33446-2305

Closest City or Town: Delray Beach, Florida

How to Get There: From I-95, take exit 52 for Atlantic Avenue westbound. Continue for approximately 4.2 miles, then turn left onto Jog Road. In about 1.3 miles, turn right onto Morikami Park Road.

GPS Coordinates: 26.4290873° N, 80.1564426° W

Best Time to Visit: Spring and fall months offer mild weather and vibrant garden blooms.

Pass/Permit/Fees: Adults: $15, Seniors: $13, Children (6-17): $9, and Children under 6: Free.

Did You Know? The museum has an impressive bonsai collection, some of which are over 100 years old.

Website:http://www.morikami.org/

DESTIN

Henderson Beach State Park

Discover the pristine beauty of Henderson Beach State Park, a coastal haven located in the vibrant city of Destin, Florida. Bask in the sun along a mile-long stretch of powder-soft white sand, bordered by emerald waters that offer an idyllic escape from the hustle and bustle of daily life.

This state park features nature trails, a playground, and picnic pavilions, making it a perfect destination for families. Experience the thrill of surf fishing, snorkeling, or simply soaking up the scenic views during a leisurely stroll.

Location: 17000 Emerald Coast Pkwy, Destin, FL 32541

Closest City or Town: Destin, Florida

How to Get There: From U.S. Highway 98, head towards Destin, and the park entrance will be clearly marked on the south side of the highway.

GPS Coordinates: 30.3847271° N, 86.4424244° W

Best Time to Visit: Late spring to early summer for optimal beach conditions.

Pass/Permit/Fees: Entrance fees: $6 per vehicle, $4 for single-occupant vehicles, and $2 for pedestrians and bicyclists.

Did You Know? Henderson Beach State Park is known for its towering sand dunes that offer unique landscapes and habitats for local wildlife.

Website: http://www.floridastateparks.org/park/Henderson-Beach

DUNEDIN

Honeymoon Island State Park

Escape to the romantic and picturesque Honeymoon Island State Park, located just off the coast of Dunedin, Florida. Known for its unspoiled beaches and rich wildlife, this barrier island truly feels like a slice of paradise.

Outdoor enthusiasts can enjoy bird-watching on the Osprey Trail, kayaking through azure waters, or simply lounging on the beach. The park also offers ferry services to nearby Caladesi Island, further enhancing your coastal adventures.

Location: 1 Causeway Blvd., Dunedin, FL 34698-8561

Closest City or Town: Dunedin, Florida

How to Get There: From downtown Dunedin, head west on Causeway Boulevard and continue over the Dunedin Causeway until you reach the park entrance.

GPS Coordinates: 28.0640795° N, 82.8304010° W

Best Time to Visit: Spring and fall for pleasant temperatures and fewer crowds.

Pass/Permit/Fees: Entrance fees: $8 per vehicle, $4 for single-occupant vehicles, and $2 for pedestrians and bicyclists.

Did You Know? Honeymoon Island was named in the 1930s after a life insurance company offered free stays on the island to newlywed couples.

Website: https://www.floridastateparks.org/park/Honeymoon-Island

EVERGLADES NATIONAL PARK

Shark Valley

Venture into the heart of the Everglades at Shark Valley, where the wild, mysterious beauty of Florida's vast wetlands comes alive. Situated in Everglades National Park, this unique destination offers an up-close look at alligators, birds, and the diverse ecosystems of the River of Grass.

Visitors can embark on a thrilling tram tour, cycle the 15-mile Shark Valley Loop, or climb the 65-foot observation tower for panoramic views of the unspoiled wilderness.

Location: Shark Valley Loop Road, Everglades National Park, FL 33194

Closest City or Town: Miami, Florida

How to Get There: From Miami, take the Tamiami Trail (U.S. Highway 41) west for about 25 miles. The entrance to Shark Valley will be on the left.

GPS Coordinates: 25.7569344° N, 80.7653560° W

Best Time to Visit: Dry season (December through April) to avoid mosquitos and enjoy cooler weather.

Pass/Permit/Fees: Entrance fees: $30 per vehicle, $25 per motorcycle, and $15 per pedestrian or cyclist. Tram tours have additional costs.

Did You Know? Despite its name, you are unlikely to find sharks in Shark Valley—it's actually a reference to the area's history and its geological shape.

Website: http://www.sharkvalleytramtours.com/

FORT LAUDERDALE

Fort Lauderdale Beach

Revel in the sun-soaked vibes at Fort Lauderdale Beach, an iconic stretch of golden sand located in the heart of Fort Lauderdale, Florida. Renowned for its sparkling waters and impressive beachfront promenade, this vacation hotspot perfectly balances relaxation and excitement.

You can indulge in various activities like parasailing, beach volleyball, or simply lounging with a good book. The nearby shopping and dining scene adds an extra layer of allure to this dynamic beach destination.

Location: A1A between Las Olas and Sunrise Blvd., Fort Lauderdale, FL 33301

Closest City or Town: Fort Lauderdale, Florida

How to Get There: Head east on Las Olas Boulevard towards the beach and follow signs for A1A. The beach is accessible from multiple entry points along A1A.

GPS Coordinates: 26.1422542° N, 80.2392612° W

Best Time to Visit: Winter months offer pleasant weather and fewer crowds.

Pass/Permit/Fees: Public beach access is free; parking fees vary depending on the location.

Did You Know? Fort Lauderdale Beach was once a popular spring break destination, famously featured in the 1960 film Where the Boys Are.

Website:https://www.parks.fortlauderdale.gov/Home/Components/ FacilityDirectory/FacilityDirectory/20/1197

Las Olas Boulevard

Discover the charm of Las Olas Boulevard, Fort Lauderdale's vibrant hub of culture, dining, and shopping. Stroll along this iconic street, lined with chic boutiques, trendy eateries, and art galleries. Nestled beside the New River, Las Olas offers an eclectic mix of experiences, from indulging in gourmet cuisine to enjoying live music. With its laid-back yet lively atmosphere, it's the perfect place to soak up the local flavor.

Location: 1032 E Las Olas Blvd, Fort Lauderdale, FL 33301

Closest City or Town: Fort Lauderdale, Florida

How to Get There: Easily accessible from downtown Fort Lauderdale, just head east on E Broward Blvd, then south on SE 8th Ave.

GPS Coordinates: 26.1190906° N, 80.1326087° W

Best Time to Visit: Early evening to enjoy both daytime shopping and evening dining.

Pass/Permit/Fees: Free to explore.

Did You Know? Las Olas Boulevard was named after its Spanish meaning "The Waves."

Website: http://lasolasboulevard.com/

FORT MYERS

Edison and Ford Winter Estates

Step into history at the Edison and Ford Winter Estates in Fort Myers. Once the winter homes of Thomas Edison and Henry Ford, these estates offer a peek into the lives of two of America's greatest innovators. Wander through the exquisite gardens, explore the historic homes, and marvel at the innovative laboratory where Edison worked on groundbreaking inventions. The estates also feature a museum rich in artifacts and exhibits.

Location: 2350 McGregor Blvd, Fort Myers, FL 33901-3315

Closest City or Town: Fort Myers, Florida

How to Get There: Head west on SR-82 (Dr Martin Luther King Jr Blvd) from downtown Fort Myers, then turn left onto McGregor Blvd.

GPS Coordinates: 26.6338939° N, 81.8800910° W

Best Time to Visit: Spring for blooming gardens and mild weather.

Pass/Permit/Fees: Adults: $25, Youth (6-12): $15, Children under 5: Free.

Did You Know? Thomas Edison planted a banyan tree on the estate in 1925 that is now one of the largest in the continental United States.

Website: http://www.edisonford.org/

Manatee Park

Connect with nature and witness one of Florida's most beloved creatures at Manatee Park. This serene refuge in Fort Myers is a designated warm-water winter haven for the West Indian Manatee. Visitors can observe these gentle giants up close from viewing platforms, especially during the colder months. The park also offers a butterfly garden, kayak rentals, and informational exhibits for a well-rounded day in nature.

Location: 10901 State Road 80, Fort Myers, FL 33905

Closest City or Town: Fort Myers, Florida

How to Get There: From I-75, take exit 141 and head east on SR-80/Palm Beach Blvd.

GPS Coordinates: 26.6931532° N, 81.7775541° W

Best Time to Visit: November to March for optimal manatee viewing.

Pass/Permit/Fees: $5 per vehicle.

Did You Know? Manatee Park is a non-captive refuge, meaning the manatees are free to come and go as they please.

Website:http://www.leegov.com/parks/Pages/FacilitySP.aspx?TermS toreId=d1b3f2ed-c99c-4e04-bdff-a1b44f047c00&TermSetId=6b286f7a-f883-4c7f-a011-5416200812c4&TermId=ab60e5d3-e722-48df-a49a-e6d5eb4d3509&UrlSuffix=manateepark

Six Mile Cypress Slough Preserve

Immerse yourself in the natural beauty of Six Mile Cypress Slough Preserve, a 3,500-acre wetland preserve in Fort Myers. Walk along the boardwalk and encounter a variety of wildlife, from alligators to wading birds, and enjoy the lush greenery and tranquil waterways. This protected area provides a peaceful retreat and a fantastic educational experience, complete with guided tours and a vibrant nature center.

Location: 7751 Penzance Blvd, Fort Myers, FL 33966-0600

Closest City or Town: Fort Myers, Florida

How to Get There: Take the Colonial Blvd exit from I-75 and head west, then turn south on Six Mile Cypress Parkway.

GPS Coordinates: 26.5705414° N, 81.8265635° W

Best Time to Visit: Winter and spring for cooler weather and active wildlife.

Pass/Permit/Fees: Individuals: $1 per hour, $5 max per vehicle.

Did You Know? The Six Mile Cypress Slough Preserve collects and naturally cleanses the water that eventually flows into Estero Bay.

Website: http://www.sloughpreserve.org/

FORT MYERS BEACH

Fort Myers Beach

Unwind at Fort Myers Beach, a stunning stretch of sand known for its breathtaking sunsets and lively atmosphere. Located on Estero Island, this beach is perfect for sunbathing, swimming, and engaging in water sports like jet skiing and parasailing. Enjoy beachfront dining, vibrant nightlife, and family-friendly attractions, making it a favorite spot for both relaxation and adventure.

Location: F322+RQ Fort Myers Beach, Florida

Closest City or Town: Fort Myers Beach, Florida

How to Get There: From Fort Myers, head south on San Carlos Blvd (SR-865) until you cross Matanzas Pass Bridge.

GPS Coordinates: 26.4520625° N, 81.9480625° W

Best Time to Visit: Late spring to early summer for sunny days and warm waters.

Pass/Permit/Fees: Access to the beach is free; parking fees vary by location.

Did You Know? Fort Myers Beach is one of the best places in Florida for spotting dolphins in their natural habitat.

Website: https://www.fortmyersbeachfl.gov/

Lovers Key State Park

Find your sense of adventure at Lovers Key State Park, a haven of natural beauty located on Estero Boulevard in Fort Myers Beach. This captivating park, which was once accessible only by boat, now welcomes visitors eager to explore its unspoiled beaches, lush mangroves, and clear blue waters. Whether you're kayaking through the tranquil backwaters, hiking the scenic trails, or spotting wildlife like manatees and dolphins, Lovers Key offers experiences that celebrate the great outdoors. One of its most unique features is the opportunity to witness spectacular sunsets from the shores, providing a picturesque end to your day.

Location: 8700 Estero Blvd, Fort Myers Beach, FL 33931-5126

Closest City or Town: Fort Myers Beach, Florida

How to Get There: From US-41, head west on Bonita Beach Road, continue onto Hickory Blvd, and follow the signs to Estero Blvd.

GPS Coordinates: 26.3913267° N, 81.8691414° W

Best Time to Visit: Spring and fall for ideal weather and fewer crowds

Pass/Permit/Fees: $8 per vehicle, $2 for pedestrians and bicyclists

Did You Know? Lovers Key was named for its romantic seclusion, making it a favorite spot for couples.

Website: https://www.floridastateparks.org/parks-and-trails/lovers-key-state-park

GRASSY KEY

Dolphin Research Center

Dive into a world of marine wonders at the Dolphin Research Center, a premier facility dedicated to the care and study of dolphins. Located in Marathon on Grassy Key, this center provides unparalleled experiences for those looking to connect with these intelligent and playful marine mammals. Participate in interactive sessions, from swimming with dolphins to learning about their behaviors and communication. The center also offers educational programs that highlight marine conservation efforts. This unique blend of adventure and education makes it a must-visit for dolphin enthusiasts.

Location: 58901 Overseas Hwy, Marathon, Grassy Key, FL 33050-6019

Closest City or Town: Marathon, Florida

How to Get There: Drive south on US-1 from Miami until you reach Mile Marker 59 on the Overseas Highway.

GPS Coordinates: 24.7669670° N, 80.9455090° W

Best Time to Visit: Year-round, but weekdays offer a more serene experience

Pass/Permit/Fees: Entrance fees vary depending on activities; visit the website for details.

Did You Know? The center was established in 1984 by delphinologists with the mission of enhancing the understanding of marine mammals.

Website: https://dolphins.org/

HOLLYWOOD

Hollywood Beach

Experience the timeless charm of Hollywood Beach, a vibrant coastal destination that merges relaxation with excitement. Located at the intersection of Jefferson Street and the Atlantic Ocean, this beach boasts pristine sandy shores, sparkling waters, and a welcoming atmosphere. Visitors can enjoy leisurely strolls along the historic Broadwalk, engage in water activities like paddleboarding, or simply relax under the sun while listening to live music from nearby venues. The unique Old Florida vibes blended with modern amenities make it a slice of paradise for beachgoers.

Location: 200 Jefferson St, Hollywood, FL 33019

Closest City or Town: Hollywood, Florida

How to Get There: From I-95, take exit 21 and head east on Sheridan Street, follow signs to A1A and turn right on Jefferson Street.

GPS Coordinates: 26.0066091° N, 80.1154529° W

Best Time to Visit: Spring and fall for perfect beach weather

Pass/Permit/Fees: Beach access is free; parking fees may apply.

Did You Know? Hollywood Beach was one of the filming locations for the classic film "Marley & Me."

Website: https://www.hollywoodfl.org/1049/Hollywood-Beach

Hollywood Beach Broadwalk

Unwind at the iconic Hollywood Beach Broadwalk, a lively 2.5-mile promenade that offers breathtaking views of the Atlantic Ocean. Situated along Hollywood's stunning coastline, this seaside strip is perfect for biking, rollerblading, or taking a leisurely stroll. With numerous cafes, shops, and live entertainment venues lining the Broadwalk, it combines the vibrancy of a boardwalk with the tranquility of a beach. Unique to this spot is the nostalgic ambiance reminiscent of old-school American beach towns, making it a beloved retreat for visitors and locals.

Location: 101 S. Broadwalk 3501 N Broadwalk, Hollywood, FL 33019-3331

Closest City or Town: Hollywood, Florida

How to Get There: From I-95, take exit 20 to Hollywood Blvd/A1A, follow signs to the Broadwalk.

GPS Coordinates: 26.0110262° N, 80.1157583° W

Best Time to Visit: Morning or late afternoon to avoid the midday heat

Pass/Permit/Fees: Access to the Broadwalk is free; parking fees vary.

Did You Know? The Hollywood Beach Broadwalk has been named one of America's Best Beach Boardwalks by Travel + Leisure magazine.

Website: https://www.floridashollywood.org/hollywood-beach-broadwalk/

JACKSONVILLE

Jacksonville Zoo & Gardens

Embark on a wild adventure at the Jacksonville Zoo & Gardens, where lush landscapes and diverse wildlife converge. Located on Zoo Parkway, this remarkable zoo is home to over 2,000 animals and 1,000 plant species spread across beautifully themed exhibits. You can wander through the African Savanna, marvel at the Great Apes, or cool off in the Wild Florida exhibit. For a hands-on experience, feed the giraffes or interact with stingrays in the touch tank. The Zoo's enchanting botanical gardens add an extra layer of beauty and tranquility to your visit.

Location: 370 Zoo Pkwy, Jacksonville, FL 32218-5770

Closest City or Town: Jacksonville, Florida

How to Get There: From I-95, take exit 358A for FL-105/Zoo Parkway, follow signs to the zoo entrance.

GPS Coordinates: 30.4040262° N, 81.6436476° W

Best Time to Visit: Spring and fall for cooler temperatures and active animals

Pass/Permit/Fees: General admission $24.95 for adults, $19.95 for children (3-12), discounts available online.

Did You Know? The Jacksonville Zoo is the only zoo in Northeast Florida.

Website: http://jacksonvillezoo.org/

KEY LARGO

John Pennekamp Coral Reef State Park

Dive into underwater wonders at John Pennekamp Coral Reef State Park, a breathtaking marine sanctuary in Key Largo, Florida. This park, renowned for its vibrant coral reefs and abundant marine life, offers an aquatic playground for snorkelers, divers, and marine enthusiasts. Experience the magic of glass-bottom boat tours, kayak through mangrove swamps, or simply relax on the pristine beaches. Unique features include the Christ of the Abyss statue submerged beneath the waves, making it a surreal and spiritual dive site.

Location: 102601 Overseas Highway, Key Largo, FL 33037

Closest City or Town: Key Largo, Florida

How to Get There: Take U.S. 1 south to Key Largo, then follow the signs to the park entrance.

GPS Coordinates: 25.1566536° N, 80.3754143° W

Best Time to Visit: Winter months (December to April) for clear weather and optimal visibility

Pass/Permit/Fees: Entrance fee is $8 per vehicle

Did You Know? John Pennekamp Coral Reef State Park is the first undersea park in the United States.

Website: https://www.floridastateparks.org/parks-and-trails/john-pennekamp-coral-reef-state-park

The Overseas Highway

Embark on a scenic adventure along The Overseas Highway, a marvel of modern engineering connecting the islands of the Florida Keys. Stretching over 113 miles from Key Largo to Key West, this highway offers stunning vistas of turquoise waters and lush landscapes. Known as the Highway that Goes to Sea, it's perfect for road trips, offering opportunities to stop at charming islands, quirky attractions, and picturesque seascapes.

FLORIDA BUCKET LIST

Location: 96000 Overseas Hwy, Key Largo, FL 33037

Closest City or Town: Key Largo, Florida

How to Get There: Start from the mainland on U.S. 1 southbound towards Key West.

GPS Coordinates: 25.0641966° N, 80.4729209° W

Best Time to Visit: Winter months for pleasant driving weather and fewer crowds

Pass/Permit/Fees: Free

Did You Know? The Overseas Highway travels over 42 bridges, including the famous Seven Mile Bridge.

Website: http://www.fla-keys.com/the-highway-that-goes-to-sea/

KEY WEST

Duval Street

Stroll through the vibrant heart of Key West along Duval Street, a bustling thoroughfare brimming with culture, history, and nightlife. From charming boutiques and art galleries to lively bars and historic landmarks, this iconic street offers a rich tapestry of experiences. Discover Hemingway's favorite haunts, savor local cuisine, and enjoy the island's laid-back atmosphere.

Location: 513 Truman Ave, Key West, FL 33040

Closest City or Town: Key West, Florida

How to Get There: Drive south on U.S. 1 to Key West, then follow signage to Duval Street.

GPS Coordinates: 24.5514980° N, 81.7988854° W

Best Time to Visit: Evenings, especially during sunsets for vibrant nightlife

Pass/Permit/Fees: Free

Did You Know? Duval Street runs from the Gulf of Mexico to the Atlantic Ocean, crossing the entire island.

Website: http://duvalstreet.net/

Fort Zachary Taylor Historic State Park

Unearth the past at Fort Zachary Taylor Historic State Park in Key West, home to a Civil War-era fort and one of Florida's favorite beach parks. Explore the historic fort, marvel at the heavy artillery, and learn about its pivotal role in American history. Beyond history, visitors can enjoy swimming, snorkeling, and picnicking against the backdrop of crystal-clear waters and white-sand beaches.

Location: 601 Howard England Way, Key West, FL 33040-8395

Closest City or Town: Key West, Florida

How to Get There: At the end of Southard Street, through the Truman Annex.

GPS Coordinates: 24.5465476° N, 81.8105646° W

Best Time to Visit: Spring and fall for comfortable weather and fewer tourists

Pass/Permit/Fees: Entrance fee is $6 per vehicle

Did You Know? The fort contains the largest collection of Civil War cannons in the country.

Website: https://www.floridastateparks.org/parks-and-trails/fort-zachary-taylor-historic-state-park

Key West Butterfly and Nature Conservatory

Immerse yourself in the fluttering beauty of the Key West Butterfly and Nature Conservatory, a tropical oasis filled with vibrant butterflies and exotic birds. Wander through lush landscapes, observe delicate butterflies alight on flowering plants, and marvel at the colorful array of winged wonders. The conservatory also features an indoor nature center with educational displays.

Location: 1316 Duval St, Key West, FL 33040-3132

Closest City or Town: Key West, Florida

How to Get There: Located on Duval Street, a short walk or bike ride from downtown Key West.

GPS Coordinates: 24.5475638° N, 81.7968249° W

Best Time to Visit: Morning hours for active butterfly sightings

Pass/Permit/Fees: Adult admission is $15

Did You Know? The conservatory is home to over 50 species of butterflies from around the world.

Website: https://keywestbutterfly.com/

Key West Lighthouse and Keeper's Quarters Museum

Find your sense of adventure at the Key West Lighthouse and Keeper's Quarters Museum, a beacon of maritime history located in

Key West, FL. This historic site invites you to explore its refurbished lighthouse tower and the keeper's quarters, offering a glimpse into the life of 19th-century lighthouse keepers. Climb the 88 steps of the lighthouse for stunning panoramic views of the island and immerse yourself in exhibits showcasing the lighthouse's storied past. Located just a short walk from Ernest Hemingway's home, this museum blends history with breathtaking scenery.

Location: 938 Whitehead St, Key West, FL 33040-7423

Closest City or Town: Key West, Florida

How to Get There: From Duval Street, head southwest on Southard Street and turn left onto Whitehead Street. The museum will be on your right.

GPS Coordinates: 24.5504565° N, 81.8006803° W

Best Time to Visit: Spring and fall for milder weather and fewer crowds

Pass/Permit/Fees: Adult admission is $15

Did You Know? The original Key West Lighthouse was built in 1825 but was destroyed by a hurricane in 1846. The current lighthouse dates back to 1848.

Website:
http://fareharbor.com/embeds/book/kwahs/items/432437/?full-items=yes&flow=879342

Mallory Square

Experience the vibrant energy of Mallory Square, a bustling waterfront destination in Key West, Florida. Famous for its nightly Sunset Celebration, Mallory Square transforms into a lively carnival at dusk, with street performers, local artisans, and food vendors coming together to bid farewell to the sun. Located at the historic heart of Key West, this square offers the perfect spot to enjoy stunning sunsets over the Gulf of Mexico while soaking in the local culture and festivities.

Location: 400 Wall St, Key West, FL 33040-6633

Closest City or Town: Key West, Florida

How to Get There: From Duval Street, head northwest on Wall Street and continue to the waterfront where you'll find Mallory Square.

GPS Coordinates: 24.5598677° N, 81.8076774° W

Best Time to Visit: Late afternoon to enjoy the Sunset Celebration

Pass/Permit/Fees: Free to explore

Did You Know? Mallory Square was named after Stephen R. Mallory, a U.S. Senator and Secretary of the Navy for the Confederate States.

Website: http://www.sunsetcelebration.org/

Mel Fisher Maritime Heritage Museum

Dive into the past at the Mel Fisher Maritime Heritage Museum, located in the cultural heart of Key West. This captivating museum showcases treasures salvaged from 17th-century shipwrecks, including gold and silver bars, coins, and religious artifacts. Named after famed treasure hunter Mel Fisher, the museum offers an immersive experience into the world of marine archaeology and shipwreck exploration. As you wander through its exhibits, you'll be transported back in time to the golden age of maritime adventures and discoveries.

Location: 200 Greene St, Key West, FL 33040-6516

Closest City or Town: Key West, Florida

How to Get There: From Duval Street, head northwest on Greene Street until you reach the museum located on your left.

GPS Coordinates: 24.5580622° N, 81.8064833° W

Best Time to Visit: Anytime, particularly on weekdays to avoid crowds

Pass/Permit/Fees: Adult admission is $16

Did You Know? The museum's collection includes artifacts from the Nuestra Señora de Atocha, a Spanish galleon that sank in 1622 and was discovered by Mel Fisher in 1985.

Website: http://www.melfisher.org/

Southernmost Point

Capture the ultimate Key West selfie at the Southernmost Point, a colorful buoy marking the southernmost tip of the continental United States. Situated at the corner of Whitehead and South streets, this iconic landmark offers a great photo opportunity with the buoy's vibrant red, yellow, and black stripes against the backdrop of the azure sea. Feel the breeze and enjoy the scenic views as you stand just 90 miles away from Cuba, making it a must-visit spot on any trip to Key West.

Location: Whitehead Street, Key West, FL 33040

Closest City or Town: Key West, Florida

How to Get There: From Duval Street, head southwest on South Street and turn right onto Whitehead Street. The Southernmost Point is at the intersection.

GPS Coordinates: 24.5465114° N, 81.7975065° W

Best Time to Visit: Early morning or late afternoon for fewer crowds

Pass/Permit/Fees: Free to visit

Did You Know? The Southernmost Point monument was established in 1983 and has since become one of the most photographed attractions in Key West.

Website: http://www.cityofkeywest-fl.gov/

The Ernest Hemingway Home and Museum

Step into literary history at The Ernest Hemingway Home and Museum, where one of America's greatest writers lived and crafted some of his most famous works. Nestled in Old Town Key West, this Spanish Colonial house is filled with Hemingway's personal belongings and remains a testament to his adventurous spirit. Explore the lush gardens, meet the six-toed cats (descendants of Hemingway's pets), and gain insight into the life and legacy of this iconic author. The home sits just a block from famous Duval Street, making it a literary oasis amidst the island's vibrant culture.

Location: 907 Whitehead Street, Key West, FL 33040-7473

Closest City or Town: Key West, Florida

How to Get There: From Duval Street, head southwest on Olivia Street and turn left onto Whitehead Street. The museum will be on your left.

GPS Coordinates: 24.5511923° N, 81.8006162° W

Best Time to Visit: Fall and winter for cooler temperatures and fewer crowds

Pass/Permit/Fees: Adult admission is $17

Did You Know? Hemingway wrote classics such as For Whom the Bell Tolls and To Have and Have Not in the studio above the carriage house.

Website: http://hemingwayhome.com/

Truman Little White House

Discover the rich history of the Truman Little White House, a presidential retreat in the heart of Key West. This historic site served as the winter White House for President Harry S. Truman, providing a unique glimpse into the lifestyle and decision-making processes of the 33rd President of the United States. Located on Front Street within a tropical paradise, visitors can tour the house, enjoy the botanical gardens, and delve into Truman's legacy. This landmark offers a blend of political history and serene landscapes, making it a must-visit for history enthusiasts.

Location: 111 Front St Naval Air Station, Key West, FL 33040-8311

Closest City or Town: Key West, Florida

How to Get There: From US-1 southbound, continue to Key West and follow signs for Truman Little White House, located within naval base territories.

GPS Coordinates: 24.5562740° N, 81.8068647° W

Best Time to Visit: Winter and spring for pleasant weather and fewer crowds.

Pass/Permit/Fees: Adults $17, Child (4-12) $8, Children under 4 free.

Did You Know? The Little White House has hosted many important meetings including the creation of the Department of Defense.

Website: http://www.trumanlittlewhitehouse.com/

KISSIMMEE

Old Town

Step back in time at Old Town, a charming entertainment district in Kissimmee. Here, the streets are lined with classic shops, vintage rides, and retro eateries, all designed to evoke the nostalgic feel of yesteryear. Stroll along the well-preserved old-fashioned streets, enjoy weekly car shows featuring vintage vehicles, and take a spin on the iconic Ferris wheel. Located on W Irlo Bronson Memorial Highway, Old Town offers a delightful blend of family fun, unique shopping, and lively events that promise to entertain visitors of all ages.

Location: 5770 W Irlo Bronson Memorial Hwy, Kissimmee, FL 34746-4732

Closest City or Town: Kissimmee, Florida

How to Get There: From I-4, take exit 64 for FL-530 E/US-192 E and follow signs to Old Town on the right.

GPS Coordinates: 28.3297765° N, 81.5156677° W

Best Time to Visit: Evenings, especially on weekends for special events.

Pass/Permit/Fees: Free to explore; ride tickets and event prices vary.

Did You Know? Old Town hosts one of America's longest-running weekly car cruises, showcasing classic cars every Saturday.

Website: http://www.myoldtownusa.com/

LOXAHATCHEE

Lion Country Safari

Embark on an unforgettable African adventure at Lion Country Safari, America's first drive-through safari park located in Loxahatchee. Spanning over 600 acres, this incredible park allows visitors to encounter wild animals like rhinos, lions, and zebras from the comfort of their own vehicle. In addition to the safari, the park features Safari World Amusement Park with giraffe feeding, water slides, and animal shows. The park offers a unique and immersive experience that brings visitors face-to-face with the wonders of the wild.

Location: 2003 Lion Country Safari Rd, Loxahatchee, FL 33470-3977

Closest City or Town: Loxahatchee, Florida

How to Get There: From I-95, take exit 68, head west on Southern Boulevard/FL-80 W, and follow the signs to Lion Country Safari.

GPS Coordinates: 26.7127391° N, 80.3222017° W

Best Time to Visit: Early mornings or weekdays to avoid crowds and heat.

Pass/Permit/Fees: Adults $37, Children (3-9) $28, under 3 free.

Did You Know? Lion Country Safari was opened in 1967 and houses over 1,000 animals.

Website: http://www.lioncountrysafari.com/

MADEIRA BEACH

John's Pass Village & Boardwalk

Dive into a coastal paradise at John's Pass Village & Boardwalk in Madeira Beach. This waterfront entertainment complex is brimming with unique shops, gourmet restaurants, and exciting attractions. Enjoy a day of shopping, dining on fresh seafood, or embarking on a dolphin-watching cruise. Located on Village Boulevard, John's Pass offers a picturesque setting where the vibrant boardwalk atmosphere meets serene water views. Whether you're seeking adventure or relaxation, this lively village has something for everyone.

Location: 12902 Village Blvd, Madeira Beach, FL 33708-2656

Closest City or Town: Madeira Beach, Florida

How to Get There: From I-275, take exit 28 to FL-694 W/Park Blvd N, continue left on Gulf Blvd to John's Pass.

GPS Coordinates: 27.7855832° N, 82.7819915° W

Best Time to Visit: Evenings and weekends for live entertainment.

Pass/Permit/Fees: Free to explore; activities vary in price.

Did You Know? John's Pass was created by a hurricane in 1848.

Website: http://www.johnspassvillage.net/

MARATHON

Seven Mile Bridge

Find your sense of adventure on the iconic Seven Mile Bridge, a breathtaking stretch of roadway spanning the Florida Keys. This engineering marvel connects Knight's Key in Marathon to Little Duck Key, offering sweeping vistas of turquoise waters along the way. Drive, bike, or walk across the bridge and experience the stunning beauty of the Gulf of Mexico and Atlantic Ocean. The bridge not only serves as a critical connection between islands but also as a scenic attraction offering unparalleled views and photo opportunities.

Location: Mile Marker 47 Overseas Hwy, Marathon, FL 33050

Closest City or Town: Marathon, Florida

How to Get There: Travel south on US-1, the bridge starts at Mile Marker 47 and stretches to Mile Marker 40.

GPS Coordinates: 24.6582654° N, 81.2858952° W

Best Time to Visit: Early mornings or late afternoons for cooler temperatures and beautiful lighting.

Pass/Permit/Fees: Free

Did You Know? The original Seven Mile Bridge built in 1912 is now a popular fishing pier and biking path.

Website: https://en.wikipedia.org/wiki/Seven_Mile_Bridge

Sombrero Beach

Discover sun-kissed bliss at Sombrero Beach, an idyllic haven located on Marathon in the Florida Keys. Renowned for its pristine white sand and turquoise waters, this beach is perfect for swimming, sunbathing, and picnicking. Located at 2150 Sombrero Beach Rd, Marathon, it offers amenities such as picnic pavilions, volleyball courts, and a playground, making it a family-friendly retreat. Unique features include its pet-friendly policy and accessible ramp for visitors with disabilities.

Location: 2150 Sombrero Beach Rd, Marathon, FL 33050

Closest City or Town: Marathon, Florida

How to Get There: From US-1, turn onto Sombrero Beach Rd and continue straight until you reach the beach.

GPS Coordinates: 24.6919500° N, 81.0850420° W

Best Time to Visit: Spring and fall for moderate temperatures and fewer crowds

Pass/Permit/Fees: Free

Did You Know? Sombrero Beach is well-known for sea turtle nesting sites; you might spot these majestic creatures or their nests during your visit.

Website: http://www.ci.marathon.fl.us/government/parks/city-parks-and-beaches/

The Turtle Hospital

Uncover marine magic with a visit to The Turtle Hospital, a unique sanctuary committed to the rehabilitation of endangered sea turtles. Nestled at 2396 Overseas Hwy, Marathon, this hospital offers educational tours where you can witness the inspiring work of rescuing and rehabilitating injured turtles. The experience provides a close-up look at these gentle creatures and fosters an appreciation for marine conservation efforts.

Location: 2396 Overseas Hwy, Marathon, FL 33050-2232

Closest City or Town: Marathon, Florida

How to Get There: Drive south on US-1 until you reach Mile Marker 48.5; the hospital is on the oceanside.

GPS Coordinates: 24.7097996° N, 81.1014172° W

Best Time to Visit: Year-round, but mornings are best to avoid the heat and catch active feeding times

Pass/Permit/Fees: Entrance fees vary; check the website for details

Did You Know? The Turtle Hospital has successfully released over 1,500 rehabilitated sea turtles back into the wild since its inception in 1986.

Website: https://www.turtlehospital.org/

MELBOURNE

Brevard Zoo

Immerse yourself in wildlife wonder at Brevard Zoo, a sprawling sanctuary housing over 900 animals across lush, naturalistic habitats. Located at 8225 N Wickham Rd, Melbourne, this zoo invites visitors to kayak through animal exhibits, zip line over enclosures, and feed giraffes by hand. Special experiences include the Treetop Trek and rafting through the African exhibit, ensuring an adventure-filled day for visitors of all ages.

Location: 8225 N Wickham Rd, Melbourne, FL 32940-7924

Closest City or Town: Melbourne, Florida

How to Get There: Easily accessible from I-95, take exit 191 and follow signs to N Wickham Rd

GPS Coordinates: 28.2249886° N, 80.7138556° W

Best Time to Visit: Spring and fall for cooler temperatures and active animals

Pass/Permit/Fees: General admission varies; check the website for up-to-date prices

Did You Know? Brevard Zoo is one of the few zoos in the U.S. where you can explore animal exhibits by kayak!

Website: http://brevardzoo.org/

MERRITT ISLAND

NASA Kennedy Space Center Visitor Complex

Blast off into an epic adventure at the NASA Kennedy Space Center Visitor Complex, where space exploration comes alive. Located on Space Commerce Way, Merritt Island, this complex offers interactive exhibits, thrilling astronaut experiences, and awe-inspiring space shuttle displays. Experience the Shuttle Launch Experience, explore the Rocket Garden, or lunch with an astronaut— every moment is a leap towards the stars.

Location: Space Commerce Way, Merritt Island, FL 32899

Closest City or Town: Merritt Island, Florida

How to Get There: Located off FL-528, follow signs to Kennedy Space Center

GPS Coordinates: 28.5218973° N, 80.6815406° W

Best Time to Visit: Year-round, but cooler months from October to April offer more comfortable weather

Pass/Permit/Fees: General admission varies; check the website for current pricing

Did You Know? The Kennedy Space Center is the launch site for every human exploration mission since 1968.

Website: http://www.kennedyspacecenter.com/

MIAMI

Bayside Marketplace

Experience the vibrant energy of Bayside Marketplace, a dynamic waterfront hub brimming with shops, dining, and entertainment options. Situated at 401 Biscayne Blvd, Miami, this bustling marketplace is a magnet for tourists and locals alike. Explore unique boutiques, savor international cuisine, or enjoy live music and boat tours offering stunning views of Miami's skyline. Bayside Marketplace has something for everyone.

Location: 401 Biscayne Blvd, Miami, FL 33132-1977

Closest City or Town: Miami, Florida

How to Get There: From I-95, take exit 2C for Miami Avenue, follow signs to Bayside Marketplace

GPS Coordinates: 25.7784025° N, 80.1867938° W

Best Time to Visit: Evenings, especially on weekends for live entertainment

Pass/Permit/Fees: Free to explore; parking and tours vary in price

Did You Know? Bayside Marketplace hosts over 150 different specialty shops, making it one of Miami's premier destinations for shopping.

Website: http://www.baysidemarketplace.com/

Jungle Island

Find your sense of adventure and wonder at Jungle Island, a lush tropical oasis nestled in the heart of Miami. This unique attraction combines the beauty of nature with interactive experiences, offering visitors the chance to get up close and personal with exotic animals like lemurs, parrots, and sloths. Whether you're navigating the zip lines, strolling through immersive aviaries, or feeding a friendly kangaroo, Jungle Island promises an unforgettable day for all ages.

Location: 1111 Parrot Jungle Trail, Miami, FL 33132-1611

Closest City or Town: Miami, Florida

How to Get There: From I-95, take exit 6B to merge onto I-395 E toward Miami Beach. Take the exit toward Watson Island and follow signs to Jungle Island.

GPS Coordinates: 25.7862070° N, 80.1750260° W

Best Time to Visit: Year-round, but early spring and late fall offer pleasant weather.

Pass/Permit/Fees: General admission starts at $27.95 for adults and $22.95 for children.

Did You Know? Jungle Island's animal ambassadors include twin orangutans, showcasing the park's dedication to wildlife conservation and education.

Website: http://www.jungleisland.com/

Little Havana

Experience the vibrant culture of Little Havana, a lively neighborhood that pulses with the rhythms of Cuban music and the aromas of authentic cuisine. Located in the heart of Miami, Little Havana is a celebration of Cuban heritage, offering visitors a taste of the island's traditions through colorful murals, bustling markets, and iconic landmarks like Domino Park. Wander along Calle Ocho, savor a Cuban coffee, and immerse yourself in the spirited atmosphere of this cultural gem.

Location: 2171 W Flagler St, Miami, FL 33135

Closest City or Town: Miami, Florida

How to Get There: From I-95, take exit 3A for FL-836 W toward Downtown, then exit at NW 12th Ave and follow signs to Little Havana.

GPS Coordinates: 25.7727149° N, 80.2304441° W

Best Time to Visit: Year-round, but visit during the Calle Ocho Festival in March for an authentic experience.

Pass/Permit/Fees: Free to explore.

Did You Know? Little Havana's Viernes Culturales (Cultural Fridays) offers free cultural events, including live music and art exhibits, on the last Friday of each month.

Website: https://www.miamiandbeaches.com/neighborhoods/little-havana

LoanDepot Park

Step into the excitement of Major League Baseball at LoanDepot Park, home to the Miami Marlins. This state-of-the-art stadium, located in the heart of Miami, features a retractable roof, ensuring a perfect game day experience regardless of the weather. Enjoy thrilling baseball action, innovative ballpark cuisine, and family-friendly entertainment. With its modern amenities and vibrant atmosphere, LoanDepot Park is the ultimate destination for sports enthusiasts.

Location: 501 Marlins Way, Miami, FL 33125-1121

Closest City or Town: Miami, Florida

How to Get There: From I-95, take exit 2B for NW 8th St, continue on W 8th St and follow signs to the ballpark.

GPS Coordinates: 25.7781487° N, 80.2195998° W

Best Time to Visit: During the baseball season (April to October) for live games.

Pass/Permit/Fees: Ticket prices vary by game; check the website for details.

Did You Know? LoanDepot Park is one of the most eco-friendly stadiums in Major League Baseball, featuring energy-efficient systems and water conservation measures.

Website: https://www.mlb.com/marlins/ballpark

Miami Seaquarium

Dive into a world of marine magic at Miami Seaquarium, an iconic oceanarium on beautiful Biscayne Bay. This family-friendly attraction offers mesmerizing shows and exhibits featuring dolphins, sea lions, and endangered manatees. Marvel at the underwater wonders in the tropical reef aquarium, enjoy hands-on experiences at the touch pools, and learn about marine conservation efforts. Miami Seaquarium is an aquatic adventure that educates and entertains.

Location: 4400 Rickenbacker Cswy, Miami, FL 33149-1032

Closest City or Town: Miami, Florida

How to Get There: From I-95, take exit 1A for FL-913 toward Key Biscayne. Follow signs to Miami Seaquarium on the Rickenbacker Causeway.

GPS Coordinates: 25.7343422° N, 80.1648178° W

Best Time to Visit: Fall and winter for cooler temperatures and fewer crowds.

Pass/Permit/Fees: General admission starts at $49.99 for adults and $39.99 for children.

Did You Know? Miami Seaquarium was the filming location for the popular 1960s TV show Flipper.

Website: http://www.miamiseaquarium.com/

Wynwood

Immerse yourself in the vibrant world of art and culture at Wynwood, Miami's dynamic arts district. Known for its colorful murals and street art, Wynwood offers an ever-changing canvas of creativity and innovation. Explore the Wynwood Walls, visit contemporary art galleries, and indulge in the district's trendy cafes and boutiques. Located in Miami, Wynwood is a neighborhood that celebrates the arts and invites visitors to experience the city's cultural heartbeat.

Location: RR22+H9 Miami, Florida

Closest City or Town: Miami, Florida

How to Get There: From I-95, take exit 2D for NW 8th St, follow NW 8th St east and turn left on NW 2nd Ave.

GPS Coordinates: 25.8014375° N, 80.1990625° W

Best Time to Visit: Year-round, but the second Saturday of each month for the Wynwood Art Walk.

Pass/Permit/Fees: Free to explore.

Did You Know? Wynwood boasts over 70 art galleries and one of the largest open-air street art installations in the world.

Website: http://wynwoodmiami.com/

Zoo Miami

Find your wild side at Zoo Miami, a sprawling sanctuary that lets visitors encounter animals from every corner of the globe. Nestled in the tropical climate of Miami, Zoo Miami is the largest and oldest zoological garden in Florida. It offers thrilling experiences like feeding giraffes, riding a camel, or hopping on a safari tram tour. Explore lush themed areas like the Amazon & Beyond and Asia, each teeming with exotic wildlife and immersive habitats. With its engaging exhibits and interactive experiences, Zoo Miami is a haven for animal lovers and adventure seekers alike.

Location: 12400 SW 152nd St, Miami, FL 33177-1402

Closest City or Town: Miami, Florida

How to Get There: From US-1, head west on SW 152nd St until you reach the zoo entrance.

GPS Coordinates: 25.6095318° N, 80.3964056° W

Best Time to Visit: Cooler months from November to April

Pass/Permit/Fees: Entrance fee is $22.95 for adults, $18.95 for children (3-12)

Did You Know? Zoo Miami covers nearly 750 acres, making it one of the largest zoos in the U.S.

Website: http://www.zoomiami.org/

Zoological Wildlife Foundation

Unleash your inner explorer at the Zoological Wildlife Foundation, where intimate animal encounters and conservation awareness go hand in hand. Located in the heart of Miami, this foundation offers a unique opportunity to interact with exotic animals like lemurs, sloths, and big cats. Guided tours provide in-depth knowledge about the animals and conservation efforts. For an unforgettable experience, opt for encounters that allow you to feed and hold various wildlife species. This sanctuary is dedicated to educating the public on wildlife conservation while offering up-close and personal animal experiences.

Location: 16225 SW 172nd Ave, Miami, FL 33187

Closest City or Town: Miami, Florida

How to Get There: From FL-874, take it to SW 149th Terrace and follow the signs to SW 172nd Ave.

GPS Coordinates: 25.6140329° N, 80.4705088° W

Best Time to Visit: Year-round, with booked tours to avoid Miami's heat

Pass/Permit/Fees: Tours range from $85 to $220; prices vary based on the experience

Did You Know? The foundation has successfully bred endangered species like the Bengal tiger and the Grevy's zebra.

Website: http://www.zwfmiami.com/

MIAMI BEACH

Art Deco Historic District

Step back in time and experience the retro charm of the Art Deco Historic District, a world-renowned treasure trove of 1930s architecture. Located in Miami Beach, this district is famed for its pastel-colored buildings adorned with neon lights and intricate facades. Enjoy a guided walking tour to understand the history and significance behind these iconic structures. The district stretches along Ocean Drive, offering a scenic backdrop of palm trees and the Atlantic Ocean. It's an architectural paradise for history buffs, art lovers, and anyone with an appreciation for beautiful, vintage aesthetics.

Location: 1001 Ocean Dr, Miami Beach, FL 33139

Closest City or Town: Miami Beach, Florida

How to Get There: From I-195, take Exit 5 for Alton Rd S, then turn left on 11th St toward Ocean Dr.

GPS Coordinates: 25.7802580° N, 80.1305038° W

Best Time to Visit: Year-round; evenings for neon lights

Pass/Permit/Fees: Free to explore; guided tours available at a fee

Did You Know? The district has over 800 historic buildings, making it the largest collection of Art Deco architecture in the world.

Website: http://www.mdpl.org/

Española Way

Find your sense of spirit and culture on Española Way, a charming pedestrian street in the heart of Miami Beach. Inspired by Mediterranean villages, this vibrant enclave bursts with life through its colorful buildings, street performers, and eclectic mix of shops and restaurants. Enjoy alfresco dining under twinkling lights, explore art galleries, or simply soak in the lively atmosphere. Located just a block from Lincoln Road, Española Way offers a quaint and delightful escape from the bustling city, making it a must-visit for anyone craving an authentic, local experience.

Location: 1436 Drexel Ave, Miami Beach, FL 33139

Closest City or Town: Miami Beach, Florida

How to Get There: From FL-907, take 14th St to Drexel Ave.

GPS Coordinates: 25.7868328° N, 80.1331226° W

Best Time to Visit: Evening to night for vibrant nightlife

Pass/Permit/Fees: Free to explore

Did You Know? Española Way was originally conceived in the 1920s as an artists' colony and is now a thriving cultural hub.

Website: http://visitespanolaway.com/

Holocaust Memorial Miami Beach

Pay homage to history at the Holocaust Memorial Miami Beach, a somber and poignant tribute located just off Meridian Avenue. This stunning outdoor sculpture garden commemorates the six million Jewish victims of the Holocaust through a series of powerful art installations and inscriptions. The centerpiece is a towering arm reaching skyward, adorned with tragic human figures. Visitors can stroll through the serene pathways, reflecting on the past and absorbing the memorial's moving message of remembrance and resilience. It's a heart-wrenching yet essential visit for anyone in Miami Beach.

Location: 1933-1945 Meridian Ave, Miami Beach, FL 33139-1817

Closest City or Town: Miami Beach, Florida

How to Get There: From I-195, exit at Alton Rd S, continue onto Dade Blvd, and turn left onto Meridian Ave.

GPS Coordinates: 25.7954768° N, 80.1362109° W

Best Time to Visit: Morning or late afternoon for a peaceful visit

Pass/Permit/Fees: Free

Did You Know? The memorial features a Wall of Hope with the names of individuals and families who perished in the Holocaust.

Website: http://holocaustmemorialmiamibeach.org/

Lincoln Road

Find your sense of exploration on Lincoln Road, Miami Beach's premier outdoor mall and dining hotspot. Spanning ten blocks, this vibrant pedestrian-only road invites visitors to indulge in shopping, dining, and people-watching in a uniquely urban atmosphere. Lined with boutique stores, top-notch restaurants, and lively street performances, Lincoln Road perfectly blends cosmopolitan flair with beach town vibes, making it an unmissable destination in Miami Beach.

Location: Lincoln Road, Miami Beach, FL 33139

Closest City or Town: Miami Beach, Florida

How to Get There: From I-195 E, take Exit 5 for Alton Road S. Continue to 17th Street, then turn left and follow signs to Lincoln Road.

GPS Coordinates: 25.7907315° N, 80.1318217° W

Best Time to Visit: Evening for a bustling atmosphere and cooler temperatures

Pass/Permit/Fees: Free to explore

Did You Know? Lincoln Road was designed by famous architect Morris Lapidus, who also designed the iconic Fontainebleau Hotel.

Website: http://www.lincolnroad.com/

Miami Beach Boardwalk

Take a leisurely stroll or an invigorating bike ride on the Miami Beach Boardwalk, where scenic ocean views meet a lively atmosphere. This 4-mile wooden pathway meanders from Indian Beach Park to South Pointe, providing an inviting space for exercise, relaxation, or simply enjoying the coastal breeze. The boardwalk's proximity to major hotels and cafes makes it a convenient yet picturesque escape in Miami Beach.

Location: 4601 Collins Ave, Miami Beach, FL 33140

Closest City or Town: Miami Beach, Florida

How to Get There: From I-195 E, take Exit 5 to Alton Road, continue to Collins Avenue and follow signage to access points.

GPS Coordinates: 25.8209129° N, 80.1215710° W

Best Time to Visit: Morning or late afternoon to avoid the midday heat

Pass/Permit/Fees: Free

Did You Know? The Miami Beach Boardwalk stretches through some of the city's most iconic districts, including the vibrant Art Deco Historic District.

Website: http://www.miamibeachboardwalk.com/

Ocean Drive

Dive into the heart of South Beach on Ocean Drive, where Art Deco architecture meets a vibrant social scene. This famous stretch is lined with pastel-colored buildings, trendy cafes, and bustling nightlife, offering a quintessential Miami experience. Located steps from the ocean, Ocean Drive is a hub of activity day and night, ideal for beachgoers, foodies, and nightlife enthusiasts.

Location: Ocean Dr, Miami Beach, FL 33139

Closest City or Town: Miami Beach, Florida

How to Get There: From I-395 E, continue onto MacArthur Causeway, turn right onto 5th Street, and left onto Ocean Drive.

GPS Coordinates: 25.7744703° N, 80.1317995° W

Best Time to Visit: Evening for a lively atmosphere and bustling nightlife

Pass/Permit/Fees: Free

Did You Know? Ocean Drive is home to the famous Colony Hotel and the Versace Mansion, hotspots for celebrity sightings.

Website: https://en.wikipedia.org/wiki/Ocean_Drive_(South_Beach)

South Pointe Park

Find your sense of tranquility at South Pointe Park, a serene escape at the southern tip of Miami Beach. This 17-acre park offers panoramic views of the Atlantic Ocean and Biscayne Bay, along with lush landscapes, walking trails, and fishing piers. An idyllic spot for picnics, casual strolls, or simply watching the cruise ships drift by, it's a must-visit for anyone seeking a peaceful retreat.

Location: 1 Washington Avenue, Miami Beach, FL 33139-7323

Closest City or Town: Miami Beach, Florida

How to Get There: From I-95 S, take Exit 2 to Alton Road South, continue to Washington Ave, and follow signs to the park.

GPS Coordinates: 25.7657952° N, 80.1341136° W

Best Time to Visit: Late afternoon for stunning sunset views

Pass/Permit/Fees: Free

Did You Know? South Pointe Park offers a direct view of Fisher Island, one of the wealthiest zip codes in the United States.

Website: https://www.miamibeachfl.gov/city-hall/parks-and-recreation/parks-facilities-directory/south-pointe-park/

NAPLES

Fifth Avenue South

Step into a world of elegance on Fifth Avenue South, the crown jewel of Naples' shopping and dining scene. This charming boulevard boasts a mix of upscale boutiques, gourmet restaurants, and art galleries, all framed by beautifully landscaped streets. Whether you're enjoying a leisurely meal al fresco or exploring unique shops, Fifth Avenue South offers a sophisticated yet laid-back experience that captures the essence of Naples.

Location: 649 5th Ave S, Naples, FL 34102-6601

Closest City or Town: Naples, Florida

How to Get There: From I-75 S, take Exit 105 to Golden Gate Pkwy, continue to 8th Street S, and turn right onto 5th Avenue S.

GPS Coordinates: 26.1417989° N, 81.7982215° W

Best Time to Visit: Evening to experience the vibrant nightlife

Pass/Permit/Fees: Free to explore

Did You Know? Fifth Avenue South features the Sugden Community Theatre, a local arts hub offering live performances year-round.

Website: https://www.facebook.com/105582384120235

Lowdermilk Beach

Find your sense of relaxation at Lowdermilk Beach, a serene and picturesque shoreline in Naples, Florida. Unwind to the sound of gentle waves as you explore this beautiful beachfront park with outstanding facilities for picnicking, sand volleyball, and gazing at the tranquil Gulf of Mexico. Located along Gulf Shore Blvd N, this cherished local spot invites you to enjoy a day by the sea, whether you're building sandcastles, swimming in the warm waters, or simply lounging under the Florida sun.

Location: 1301 Gulf Shore Blvd N, Naples, FL 34102-4980

Closest City or Town: Naples, Florida

How to Get There: From US-41, head west on 14th Ave N and turn right onto Gulf Shore Blvd N to reach the beach.

GPS Coordinates: 26.1620540° N, 81.8099780° W

Best Time to Visit: Year-round, with fewer crowds in early mornings or late afternoons

Pass/Permit/Fees: Metered parking rates apply.

Did You Know? Lowdermilk Beach features a gazebo available for rental, making it a charming spot for beachside gatherings.

Website: https://www.naplesgov.com/parksrec/park/lowdermilk-park

Naples Botanical Garden

Immerse yourself in the natural beauty of the Naples Botanical Garden, a vibrant oasis showcasing the diverse flora of the tropics and subtropics. Located on Bayshore Dr, this renowned garden spans 170 acres and features themed gardens that reflect ecosystems from around the world. Experience the tranquility of the Butterfly House, marvel at exotic plants, and learn about sustainable gardening practices. It's a place where nature and artistry combine to create breathtaking landscapes.

Location: 4820 Bayshore Dr, Naples, FL 34112-7336

Closest City or Town: Naples, Florida

How to Get There: From US-41, head east on Thomasson Dr, then turn right onto Bayshore Dr to reach the garden.

GPS Coordinates: 26.1068493° N, 81.7710701° W

Best Time to Visit: Winter and spring for vibrant blooms and cooler weather

Pass/Permit/Fees: General admission: $20 for adults, $10 for children (4-14)

Did You Know? The Naples Botanical Garden features a dedicated Children's Garden, offering interactive experiences for young nature enthusiasts.

Website: https://www.naplesgarden.org/

Naples Pier

Find your sense of history and serenity at the Naples Pier, a beloved landmark dating back to 1888. Stretching 1,000 feet into the Gulf of Mexico, this iconic pier offers stunning views, excellent fishing opportunities, and a chance to spot dolphins frolicking in the waves. Located at the end of 12th Ave S, it's more than just a pier—it's a slice of Naples history and a perfect spot for sunset viewing or a leisurely stroll.

Location: 45JV+J2 Naples, Florida

Closest City or Town: Naples, Florida

How to Get There: From US-41, take 12th Ave S west until you reach the pier.

GPS Coordinates: 26.1315895° N, 81.8073328° W

Best Time to Visit: Sunset for stunning views and cooler temperatures

Pass/Permit/Fees: Free

Did You Know? The Naples Pier has undergone numerous restorations due to hurricanes, but remains a vital piece of the city's heritage.

Website: https://www.naplesgov.com/parksrec/page/naples-pier

Naples Zoo at Caribbean Gardens

Embark on a wild adventure at Naples Zoo at Caribbean Gardens, where exotic animals and lush botanicals come together in a historic setting. Located on Goodlette-Frank Rd, this AZA-accredited zoo features exciting exhibits like the Primate Expedition Cruise, where you can see monkeys and apes in their naturalistic island habitats. With daily animal shows, zookeeper talks, and lush garden pathways, it's an education and adventure experience for all ages.

Location: 1590 Goodlette-Frank Rd, Naples, FL 34102-5260

Closest City or Town: Naples, Florida

How to Get There: From US-41, head north on Goodlette-Frank Rd to reach the zoo entrance.

GPS Coordinates: 26.1694770° N, 81.7878043° W

Best Time to Visit: Mornings for active animals and cooler weather

Pass/Permit/Fees: General admission: $22.95 for adults, $14.95 for children (3-12)

Did You Know? Naples Zoo is home to rare species like the fosa, Madagascar's top predator, which is rarely seen in other U.S. zoos.

Website: http://www.napleszoo.org/

ORLANDO

Aquatica

Dive into fun and thrills at Aquatica, SeaWorld's water park in Orlando, Florida. Located on Water Play Way, this exciting water park features exhilarating water slides, wave pools, and lazy rivers. Enjoy the unique Dolphin Plunge, where riders slide through clear tubes surrounded by playful Commerson's dolphins. It's the perfect destination for families and thrill-seekers alike, offering a blend of relaxation and adrenaline-pumping attractions.

Location: 5800 Water Play Way, Orlando, FL 32821

Closest City or Town: Orlando, Florida

How to Get There: From I-4, take Exit 71 toward Central Florida Pkwy and follow signs to the park.

GPS Coordinates: 28.4158642° N, 81.4562899° W

Best Time to Visit: Spring and early summer for warm weather and fewer crowds

Pass/Permit/Fees: General admission: Prices vary; check the website for seasonal rates.

Did You Know? Aquatica is home to Roa's Rapids, a fast-paced, action-packed version of a lazy river that takes you through geysers and waterfalls.

Website: https://aquatica.com/orlando/

Cinderella Castle

Find your sense of wonder at Cinderella Castle, the enchanting centerpiece of Magic Kingdom Park in Orlando, Florida. Symbolizing the magic and fantasy that Disney is known for, this iconic landmark draws visitors from around the world. Located in Fantasyland, the castle offers a range of experiences, from delightful dining at Cinderella's Royal Table to breathtaking views from the surrounding gardens. Watch enchanting fireworks light up the sky, or meet beloved Disney characters for a truly magical moment. Its majestic spires and fairytale design make it a must-see for anyone visiting Walt Disney World.

Location: 1180 Seven Seas Drive Fantasyland at Magic Kingdom Park, Orlando, FL 32836

Closest City or Town: Orlando, Florida

How to Get There: From I-4, take exit 67 to World Drive. Follow signage to Magic Kingdom Park. The castle is centrally located within the park.

GPS Coordinates: 28.4193576° N, 81.5811934° W

Best Time to Visit: Early mornings or late evenings for fewer crowds

Pass/Permit/Fees: Requires a Walt Disney World ticket; prices vary

Did You Know? Cinderella Castle stands at 189 feet tall and features 27 towers.

Website: https://disneyworld.disney.go.com/attractions/magic-kingdom/cinderella-castle/

Discovery Cove

Immerse yourself in a tropical paradise at Discovery Cove, an all-inclusive day resort in Orlando, Florida. Swim with dolphins, snorkel with tropical fish, and hand-feed exotic birds in a serene, lush environment. Located on Discovery Cove Way, this unique destination offers experiences that blend adventure with relaxation. Enjoy unlimited food and beverages, relaxing on sandy beaches, or floating along the Wind-Away River. Discovery Cove's exceptional animal encounters and luxurious amenities make it a must-visit for nature and adventure lovers alike.

Location: 6000 Discovery Cove Way, Orlando, FL 32821-6000

Closest City or Town: Orlando, Florida

How to Get There: From I-4, take exit 71 for SeaWorld Drive, follow the signs to Discovery Cove.

GPS Coordinates: 28.4050865° N, 81.4624541° W

Best Time to Visit: Spring and fall for pleasant weather

Pass/Permit/Fees: All-inclusive admission starts at $211; advance reservations required

Did You Know? Discovery Cove's dolphin lagoon holds over a million gallons of seawater.

Website: http://discoverycove.com/orlando/

Disney's Animal Kingdom Theme Park

Unleash your wild side at Disney's Animal Kingdom Theme Park, a spectacular blend of nature, adventure, and imagination in Orlando, Florida. Covering 580 acres, this park houses more than 2,000 animals and features themed areas like Pandora – The World of Avatar. Located on Osceola Parkway, it offers thrilling rides, such as Expedition Everest and Kilimanjaro Safaris, where visitors can see free-roaming wildlife. Unique immersive experiences like the Festival of the Lion King and the Tree of Life bring stories alive in unforgettable ways.

Location: 2901 Osceola Pkwy, Orlando, FL 32830-8410

Closest City or Town: Orlando, Florida

How to Get There: From I-4, take exit 65 for Osceola Parkway. Follow signs to Disney's Animal Kingdom Theme Park.

GPS Coordinates: 28.3574423° N, 81.5905788° W

Best Time to Visit: Weekdays during the off-season (January, February, September)

Pass/Permit/Fees: Requires a Walt Disney World ticket; prices vary

Did You Know? The park's iconic Tree of Life features over 300 intricately carved animal sculptures.

Website: http://disneyworld.disney.go.com/parks/animal-kingdom/?CMP=OKC-wdw_TA_118

Disney's Blizzard Beach Water Park

Dive into a snowy oasis at Disney's Blizzard Beach Water Park, a fun-filled destination in Orlando, Florida. Set in a melting ski resort theme, this unique water park offers thrilling rides like Summit Plummet, one of the world's tallest and fastest free-fall body slides. Located on West Buena Vista Drive, the park also features a relaxing wave pool, lazy river, and kid-friendly areas like Tike's Peak for little adventurers. With its imaginative design and cool activities, Blizzard Beach offers a refreshing escape from the Florida heat.

Location: 1801 West Buena Vista Drive, Orlando, FL 32830-8436

Closest City or Town: Orlando, Florida

How to Get There: From I-4, take exit 64 for US-192 West toward Magic Kingdom. Follow signs to Blizzard Beach Water Park.

GPS Coordinates: 28.3394476° N, 81.5728815° W

Best Time to Visit: Spring and early summer before peak crowds

Pass/Permit/Fees: Requires a Walt Disney World ticket; prices vary

Did You Know? Blizzard Beach holds the title for the highest artificially created waterfall in the world at 120 feet.

Website: http://disneyworld.disney.go.com/parks/blizzard-beach/?CMP=OKC-wdw_TA_36

Disney's Typhoon Lagoon Water Park

Plunge into fun and adventure at Disney's Typhoon Lagoon Water Park, a tropical-themed water wonderland in Orlando, Florida. Centered around a massive wave pool, the park features exhilarating water slides like Humunga Kowabunga and the Crush 'n' Gusher water coaster. Located on East Buena Vista Boulevard, it offers sandy beaches, a lazy river, and snorkeling with tropical fish at Shark Reef. With its lush scenery and wave-filled excitement, Typhoon Lagoon is perfect for cooling off and creating splash-tastic memories.

Location: 1145 East Buena Vista Boulevard, Orlando, FL 32830

Closest City or Town: Orlando, Florida

How to Get There: From I-4, take exit 68 to State Route 535 N. Follow Disney signs to Typhoon Lagoon.

GPS Coordinates: 28.3662991° N, 81.5284281° W

Best Time to Visit: Summer months for full ride availability

Pass/Permit/Fees: Requires a Walt Disney World ticket; prices vary

Did You Know? The park's wave pool can generate six-foot waves and is one of the largest in the world.

Website: http://disneyworld.disney.go.com/parks/typhoon-lagoon/?CMP=OKC-wdw_TA_37

Epcot

Explore a world of innovation and culture at Epcot, a fascinating theme park situated in the heart of the Walt Disney World Resort in Orlando, Florida. Epcot invites visitors to journey across Future World, showcasing cutting-edge technology and visions of tomorrow, and World Showcase, an incredible collection of pavilions representing 11 countries. From thrilling attractions like Soarin' Around the World to immersive cultural experiences and delicious international cuisine, Epcot offers a unique blend of education and entertainment for all ages.

Location: 200 EPCOT Center Dr Walt Disney World Resort, Orlando, FL 32830

Closest City or Town: Orlando, Florida

How to Get There: Accessible via I-4; follow signs for Epcot within Walt Disney World Resort.

GPS Coordinates: 28.3764687° N, 81.5494034° W

Best Time to Visit: Weekdays during the off-season months (January, February, September)

Pass/Permit/Fees: Admission requires a Walt Disney World ticket; prices vary.

Did You Know? Epcot stands for Experimental Prototype Community of Tomorrow, reflecting Walt Disney's vision for a futuristic city.

Website: https://disneyworld.disney.go.com/destinations/epcot/

Fun Spot America Orlando

Find your sense of excitement and adventure at Fun Spot America Orlando, a thrilling amusement park located in Orlando, Florida. This family-friendly park offers a variety of rides, from heart-pounding roller coasters to classic go-karts and a vast arcade. Located just minutes from International Drive, Fun Spot provides unlimited fun with unique attractions like the world's tallest skycoaster and interactive funhouses, ensuring a memorable experience for all ages.

Location: 5700 Fun Spot Way, Orlando, FL 32819-0001

Closest City or Town: Orlando, Florida

How to Get There: From I-4, take exit 75A towards International Dr., follow signs to Fun Spot America Orlando.

GPS Coordinates: 28.4654176° N, 81.4555573° W

Best Time to Visit: Spring and fall for milder weather and fewer crowds

Pass/Permit/Fees: Entrance is free; ride tickets and unlimited armbands are available for purchase.

Did You Know? Fun Spot America Orlando is home to White Lightning, the only wooden roller coaster in Orlando.

Website: http://fun-spot.com/

Happily Ever After Fireworks

End your day with awe and wonder at the Happily Ever After Fireworks, a spectacular nighttime show at Magic Kingdom Park in Orlando, Florida. This dazzling display combines fireworks, projections, and music to bring beloved Disney stories to life against the backdrop of Cinderella Castle. Located within the enchanting Magic Kingdom, the show promises a magical experience that captures the essence of Disney's fairy tales, making it a perfect finale to your visit.

Location: 1180 7 Seas Dr Magic Kingdom Park, Orlando, FL 32830

Closest City or Town: Orlando, Florida

How to Get There: Follow signs to Magic Kingdom from I-4 or World Drive; park using the Transportation and Ticket Center.

GPS Coordinates: 28.4048775° N, 81.5803605° W

Best Time to Visit: Evenings during weekdays for lower crowds

Pass/Permit/Fees: Requires a Walt Disney World ticket; prices vary.

Did You Know? The Happily Ever After Fireworks show features more than 18 minutes of pyrotechnics and projection mapping.

Website: http://disneyworld.disney.go.com/entertainment/magic-kingdom/happily-ever-after-fireworks/

International Drive

Discover the vibrant pulse of Orlando on International Drive, the city's premier dining and entertainment district. Known as I-Drive, this bustling thoroughfare is lined with world-class attractions, restaurants, and shopping centers. Stretching through the heart of Orlando, visitors can enjoy theme parks, indoor skydiving, live shows, and much more. International Drive offers endless fun and excitement, making it a must-visit for tourists and locals alike.

Location: 7081 Grand National Drive, Orlando, FL 32819-8112

Closest City or Town: Orlando, Florida

How to Get There: From I-4, take exit 74A, head east on Sand Lake Rd, and follow signs to International Drive.

GPS Coordinates: 28.4748270° N, 81.4518714° W

Best Time to Visit: Evenings or weekends for a lively atmosphere

Pass/Permit/Fees: Free to explore; attraction fees vary.

Did You Know? International Drive is home to ICON Park, featuring The Wheel, a 400-foot tall observation wheel offering spectacular views of Orlando.

Website: http://www.internationaldriveorlando.com/

Kia Center

Experience the thrill of top-tier basketball and world-class concerts at the Kia Center, a dynamic multi-purpose arena in Orlando, Florida. Home to the Orlando Magic NBA team, this state-of-the-art venue hosts a wide variety of events, from high-energy sports games to renowned music performances. Located downtown, the Kia Center's modern amenities and central location make it a premier destination for entertainment in Orlando.

Location: 400 W Church St, Orlando, FL 32801-2515

Closest City or Town: Orlando, Florida

How to Get There: From I-4, take exit 82B for South St, turn left onto Church St, and the Kia Center will be on your left.

GPS Coordinates: 28.5392214° N, 81.3838535° W

Best Time to Visit: Year-round, depending on event schedule

Pass/Permit/Fees: Ticket prices vary by event; check the website for details.

Did You Know? The Kia Center can accommodate up to 20,000 spectators, making it one of the largest arenas in Florida.

Website: http://kiacenter.com/

Madame Tussauds Orlando

Step into the glittering world of celebrity at Madame Tussauds Orlando, where lifelike wax figures of your favorite stars await. Located on International Drive, this famed museum offers a chance to pose with incredibly detailed figures of A-list celebrities, historic icons, and pop culture legends. From Hollywood stars to sports heroes, the array of figures provides a fun and interactive experience for visitors of all ages. Be part of the action in themed rooms that create the perfect backdrop for unforgettable selfies and memories.

Location: 8387 International Drive, Orlando, FL 32819-9300

Closest City or Town: Orlando, Florida

How to Get There: From I-4, take exit 74A, head east on Sand Lake Road, then turn right onto International Drive.

GPS Coordinates: 28.4437626° N, 81.4686057° W

Best Time to Visit: Weekdays to avoid crowds

Pass/Permit/Fees: General admission starts at $29.95; various combination tickets available.

Did You Know? Madame Tussauds has been crafting wax figures for over 200 years, starting with Marie Tussaud's sculptures in the 18th century.

Website: http://www.madametussauds.com/Orlando

SEA LIFE Orlando Aquarium

Dive into an underwater adventure at SEA LIFE Orlando Aquarium, where you can explore vibrant marine habitats and encounter stunning sea creatures. Located on International Drive, this immersive aquarium offers interactive exhibits that bring you face-to-face with sharks, rays, and colorful tropical fish. Wander through the mesmerizing ocean tunnel, discover the wonders of jellyfish, and learn about marine conservation efforts in a family-friendly setting.

Location: 8449 International Dr, Orlando, FL 32819-9300

Closest City or Town: Orlando, Florida

How to Get There: From I-4, take exit 74A, head east on Sand Lake Road, then turn right onto International Drive.

GPS Coordinates: 28.4425885° N, 81.4685680° W

Best Time to Visit: Early mornings or weekdays for fewer crowds

Pass/Permit/Fees: General admission starts at $32 for adults, $28 for children.

Did You Know? SEA LIFE Orlando features Florida's only 360-degree ocean tunnel, offering panoramic views of underwater life.

Website: http://www.visitsealife.com/orlando

SeaWorld

Embark on an unforgettable oceanic adventure at SeaWorld Orlando, where thrilling rides, stunning shows, and up-close animal encounters await. Located on SeaWorld Drive, this famous marine park combines entertainment with education, featuring attractions like the exhilarating Mako roller coaster and the inspiring Orca Encounter show. Explore interactive exhibits, enjoy live performances, and discover the diverse marine life that calls SeaWorld home.

Location: 7007 SeaWorld Drive, Orlando, FL 32821-8097

Closest City or Town: Orlando, Florida

How to Get There: From I-4, take exit 71 for Central Florida Parkway and follow signs to SeaWorld.

GPS Coordinates: 28.4111520° N, 81.4619367° W

Best Time to Visit: Spring and fall for mild weather and lower crowds

Pass/Permit/Fees: General admission starts at $79; various passes and packages available.

Did You Know? SeaWorld Orlando is home to the world's tallest river rapid drop on Infinity Falls, an exciting water ride.

Website: http://seaworld.com/orlando/

The Florida Mall

Discover a shopper's paradise at The Florida Mall, the largest shopping center in Central Florida, boasting over 250 retail stores and dining options. Situated on South Orange Blossom Trail, this expansive mall offers everything from luxury brands to popular high street stores. Families can enjoy the Crayola Experience, while fashion enthusiasts browse the latest trends. With a variety of eateries, The Florida Mall is perfect for a full day of shopping and entertainment.

Location: 8001 S Orange Blossom Trail, Orlando, FL 32809-7654

Closest City or Town: Orlando, Florida

How to Get There: From I-4, take exit 74A for Sand Lake Road, continue straight, and follow signs to South Orange Blossom Trail.

GPS Coordinates: 28.4459240° N, 81.3955090° W

Best Time to Visit: Weekdays to avoid weekend shopping crowds

Pass/Permit/Fees: Free to enter; individual store prices vary.

Did You Know? The Florida Mall spans 1.8 million square feet, making it the largest single-story mall in the United States.

Website: http://www.simon.com/mall/the-florida-mall

The Wizarding World of Harry Potter at Universal Orlando Resort

Step into the magical universe of The Wizarding World of Harry Potter at Universal Orlando Resort, where the enchanting lands of Diagon Alley and Hogsmeade bring J.K. Rowling's series to life. Located on Universal Boulevard, this immersive experience features thrilling rides, such as Harry Potter and the Forbidden Journey, and iconic landmarks like Hogwarts Castle. Explore spellbinding shops, taste authentic Butterbeer, and encounter magical creatures as you embark on an unforgettable journey.

Location: 6000 Universal Boulevard Islands Of Adventure, Orlando, FL 32819-7640

Closest City or Town: Orlando, Florida

How to Get There: From I-4, take exit 75A, follow signs to Universal Orlando Resort, and enter through the main gate.

GPS Coordinates: 28.4719507° N, 81.4684926° W

Best Time to Visit: Weekdays and off-season months (January, February, September) for shorter lines.

Pass/Permit/Fees: Requires a Universal Orlando ticket; prices vary.

Did You Know? The famous Hogwarts Express train ride connects the two sections of The Wizarding World, providing an immersive transport experience between Diagon Alley and Hogsmeade.

Website: http://www.universalorlando.com/

Tree of Life

Find your sense of awe and wonder at the Tree of Life, located in Disney's Animal Kingdom Theme Park in Orlando, Florida. This 145-foot marvel features over 300 intricately carved animal figures, serving as the park's symbolic centerpiece. Wander around its base on the Discovery Island Trails, where you'll encounter exotic wildlife and lush flora. Unique experiences include It's Tough to be a Bug, a 3D show nestled inside the tree. It's not just an attraction, it's a stunning tribute to the diversity of life on Earth.

Location: 2901 Osceola Pkwy Disney's Animal Kingdom Theme Park, Orlando, FL 32830

Closest City or Town: Orlando, Florida

How to Get There: From I-4, take exit 65 for Osceola Parkway. Follow signs to Disney's Animal Kingdom Theme Park.

GPS Coordinates: 28.3578902° N, 81.5906207° W

Best Time to Visit: Spring and fall for pleasant weather.

Pass/Permit/Fees: Requires a Walt Disney World ticket; prices vary.

Did You Know? The Tree of Life contains about 8,000 branches and 102,000 artificial leaves.

Website: https://disneyworld.disney.go.com/attractions/animal-kingdom/tree-of-life/

Universal Islands of Adventure

Find your sense of thrill and exploration at Universal Islands of Adventure, located in Orlando, Florida. This action-packed theme park features awe-inspiring lands like Marvel Super Hero Island, The Wizarding World of Harry Potter, and Jurassic Park. Plunge down water rides, soar on coasters, and meet iconic characters. Explore the unique attractions like The Incredible Hulk Coaster and Harry Potter and the Forbidden Journey. Each island promises a new adventure and endless excitement.

Location: 6000 Universal Blvd, Orlando, FL 32819-7640

Closest City or Town: Orlando, Florida

How to Get There: Accessible via I-4; take exit 75A for Universal Blvd, follow signs to Universal Islands of Adventure.

GPS Coordinates: 28.4716879° N, 81.4701971° W

Best Time to Visit: Weekdays and off-peak seasons (January, February, September) to avoid crowds.

Pass/Permit/Fees: Requires an admission ticket; prices vary.

Did You Know? The park's Hulk roller coaster accelerates from 0 to 40 mph in just 2 seconds!

Website: https://www.universalorlando.com/web/en/us/theme-parks/islands-of-adventure

Universal Studios Florida

Step into the excitement of movie magic at Universal Studios Florida, situated in Orlando. The park offers exhilarating attractions based on beloved films and shows, from The Simpsons to Transformers. Located on Universal Boulevard, it features thrilling rides, interactive shows, and behind-the-scenes glimpses into the filmmaking process. Unique features like Diagon Alley from the Wizarding World of Harry Potter and the Hollywood Rip Ride Rockit coaster ensure a day filled with adventure.

Location: 6000 Universal Boulevard, Orlando, FL 32819-7640

Closest City or Town: Orlando, Florida

How to Get There: Accessible via I-4; take exit 75A for Universal Blvd, then follow signs to Universal Studios.

GPS Coordinates: 28.4739842° N, 81.4653768° W

Best Time to Visit: Weekdays and off-peak seasons for shorter wait times.

Pass/Permit/Fees: Requires an admission ticket; prices vary.

Did You Know? Universal Studios Florida was the first park in the Universal Orlando Resort, opening in 1990.

Website: https://www.universalorlando.com/web/en/us/theme-parks/universal-studios-florida

Universal Volcano Bay

Submerge into tropical fun at Universal Volcano Bay, a thrilling water park located in Orlando. This island oasis features exciting water rides, lazy rivers, and private cabanas. Experience the adrenaline rush of the Krakatau Aqua Coaster or relax on the sandy beaches at Waturi Beach. The park's TapuTapu wearable technology makes it easy to reserve ride times and explore at your leisure, ensuring a seamless and exhilarating experience for all ages.

Location: 6000 Universal Blvd, Orlando, FL 32819-7640

Closest City or Town: Orlando, Florida

How to Get There: Accessible via I-4; take exit 75A for Universal Blvd, follow signs to Universal Volcano Bay.

GPS Coordinates: 28.4619885° N, 81.4724528° W

Best Time to Visit: Spring and early summer for optimal weather.

Pass/Permit/Fees: Requires an admission ticket; prices vary.

Did You Know? The park's central volcano, Krakatau, stands at 200 feet tall.

Website: https://www.universalorlando.com/web/en/us/theme-parks/volcano-bay/index.html

Walt Disney World Resort

Immerse yourself in the magic at Walt Disney World Resort, an iconic destination located in Orlando, Florida. This expansive resort encompasses four theme parks, two water parks, numerous hotels, and endless entertainment options. With beloved attractions like Cinderella Castle, Space Mountain, and EPCOT's World Showcase, Walt Disney World Resort captivates visitors of all ages. From thrilling rides to enchanting shows and character meet-and-greets, the resort promises a magical experience with every visit.

Location: World Drive, Orlando, FL 32830

Closest City or Town: Orlando, Florida

How to Get There: Accessible via I-4; follow signs for Walt Disney World Resort.

GPS Coordinates: 28.3771857° N, 81.5707400° W

Best Time to Visit: Weekdays during the off-season months (January, February, September)

Pass/Permit/Fees: Requires a Walt Disney World ticket; prices vary.

Did You Know? Walt Disney World spans nearly 25,000 acres, making it roughly the size of San Francisco!

Website: http://disneyworld.disney.go.com/?CMP=OKC-wdw_TA_421

World of Disney

Find your sense of wonder at the World of Disney, the ultimate shopping destination for Disney fans in Orlando, Florida. Nestled in Disney Springs, this massive store is a treasure trove of magical merchandise, from exclusive Disney apparel to must-have collectibles. Beyond shopping, you can marvel at enchanting displays and themed decorations that make you feel like you're part of the story. Whether you're searching for the perfect souvenir or just soaking in the Disney magic, this expansive retail experience promises something special for every visitor.

Location: 1486 East Buena Vista Drive, Orlando, FL 32830

Closest City or Town: Orlando, Florida

How to Get There: From I-4, take Exit 67 to Epcot/Disney Springs. Follow signs to Disney Springs, and locate the World of Disney store in the Marketplace area.

GPS Coordinates: 28.3712879° N, 81.5150165° W

Best Time to Visit: Early morning or late evening to avoid crowds

Pass/Permit/Fees: Free to enter, merchandise prices vary

Did You Know? The World of Disney at Disney Springs is the largest Disney merchandise store in the world.

Website: https://www.disneysprings.com/shopping/world-of-disney/

PANAMA CITY

Shell Island

Discover unspoiled beauty at Shell Island, an untouched barrier island off Panama City Beach, Florida. Accessible only by boat, this pristine destination offers miles of serene white sand beaches and crystal-clear waters perfect for swimming, snorkeling, and shell collecting. Located between the Gulf of Mexico and St. Andrew Bay, Shell Island provides a tranquil escape from the bustling mainland, offering unmatched opportunities for wildlife sightings and nature exploration.

Location: 479H+FH Panama City, Florida

Closest City or Town: Panama City Beach, Florida

How to Get There: Reachable only by boat; take a shuttle from Panama City Beach Marina or launch your own boat from a nearby ramp.

GPS Coordinates: 30.1186876° N, 85.7210280° W

Best Time to Visit: Spring and fall for mild weather and fewer crowds

Pass/Permit/Fees: Free, but boat shuttle services charge various fees

Did You Know? Shell Island is a critical nesting site for endangered shorebirds and sea turtles.

Website: https://www.visitpanamacitybeach.com/things-to-do/beaches/shell-island/

PANAMA CITY BEACH

Gulf World Marine Park

Immerse yourself in marine adventures at Gulf World Marine Park in Panama City Beach, Florida. This dynamic park offers captivating shows and interactive experiences with dolphins, sea lions, and other marine life. Located along Front Beach Road, Gulf World promises educational fun through animal encounters, aquariums, and entertaining performances. It's an ideal destination for family outings, providing memorable experiences that blend excitement with marine conservation.

Location: 15412 Front Beach Rd, Panama City Beach, FL 32413-2502

Closest City or Town: Panama City Beach, Florida

How to Get There: From U.S. Highway 98, turn west onto Front Beach Road and follow the signs to Gulf World Marine Park.

GPS Coordinates: 30.2109791° N, 85.8675365° W

Best Time to Visit: Spring and summer for full show schedules

Pass/Permit/Fees: General admission: $29 for adults, $19 for children (3-11)

Did You Know? Gulf World is one of the few venues in the U.S. where visitors can swim with dolphins.

Website: http://www.gulfworldmarinepark.com/

Panama City Beach

Soak up the sun at Panama City Beach, a stunning stretch of sand along Florida's Gulf Coast. Renowned for its emerald waters and 27 miles of breathtaking beaches, this vibrant destination offers endless outdoor activities, from parasailing and jet skiing to beach volleyball and fishing. Located at S Thomas Drive, Panama City Beach is a paradise for those seeking both relaxation and adventure, with lively piers, bustling boardwalks, and serene nature trails.

Location: 9900 S Thomas Dr, Panama City Beach, FL 32408

Closest City or Town: Panama City Beach, Florida

How to Get There: From U.S. Highway 98, head south on Thomas Drive to reach the beach.

GPS Coordinates: 30.1764562° N, 85.8055901° W

Best Time to Visit: Spring and summer for prime beach weather

Pass/Permit/Fees: Free to access; parking fees vary

Did You Know? Panama City Beach hosts the annual Spring Break celebration, attracting thousands of college students each year.

Website: https://panamacitybeach.com/

St. Andrews State Park

Embark on an outdoor adventure at St. Andrews State Park, a natural haven on the Gulf Coast of Panama City Beach, Florida. This park is a playground for nature lovers, offering activities such as hiking, snorkeling, and fishing. Located at State Park Lane, it features pristine beaches, lush pine forests, and a rich variety of wildlife. Unique experiences include renting a kayak to explore the tidal inlets or taking a shuttle to the neighboring Shell Island.

Location: 4607 State Park Lane, Panama City Beach, FL 32408-7347

Closest City or Town: Panama City Beach, Florida

How to Get There: From U.S. Highway 98, head south on Thomas Drive and follow signs to the park entrance.

GPS Coordinates: 30.1314437° N, 85.7365997° W

Best Time to Visit: Spring and fall for pleasant temperatures and fewer crowds

Pass/Permit/Fees: Entrance fee: $8 per vehicle

Did You Know? St. Andrews State Park was once a military reservation during World War II.

Website: https://www.floridastateparks.org/parks-and-trails/st-andrews-state-park

PENSACOLA BEACH

Pensacola Beach

Find your sense of relaxation and adventure at Pensacola Beach, a stunning stretch of sand along Florida's Emerald Coast. Known for its sugar-white sands and crystal-clear turquoise waters, this beach offers a range of activities from sunbathing and swimming to sailing and snorkeling. Located on Santa Rosa Island, Pensacola Beach combines the tranquility of the Gulf of Mexico with lively beachfront bars and eateries. It's the perfect spot to soak up the sun, dive into water sports, and enjoy vibrant nightlife, making it an ultimate beach destination.

Location: Pensacola Beach Blvd, Pensacola Beach, FL 32561

Closest City or Town: Pensacola Beach, Florida

How to Get There: From US-98, take the FL-399 east exit toward Pensacola Beach. Follow the signs to the bridge that leads straight to the beach.

GPS Coordinates: 30.3482886° N, 87.1537060° W

Best Time to Visit: Spring and fall for pleasant weather and fewer crowds

Pass/Permit/Fees: Beach access is free; parking fees may apply.

Did You Know? Pensacola Beach is part of the Gulf Islands National Seashore, offering protected landscapes and abundant wildlife.

Website: https://visitpensacolabeach.com/

PONCE INLET

Ponce De Leon Inlet Lighthouse & Museum

Embark on a historical journey at the Ponce De Leon Inlet Lighthouse & Museum, standing tall at the tip of the Ponce de Leon Inlet in Florida. This towering beacon, built in 1887, is the tallest lighthouse in Florida and one of the tallest in the country. Situated in Ponce Inlet, visitors can climb the 203 steps to the top for breathtaking views of the Atlantic Ocean and the Intracoastal Waterway. Explore the well-preserved keeper's quarters, maritime exhibits, and original Fresnel lens, making for an educational and awe-inspiring visit.

Location: 4931 S Peninsula Dr, Ponce Inlet, FL 32127-7301

Closest City or Town: Ponce Inlet, Florida

How to Get There: From I-95, take exit 256 toward Daytona Beach, turn right onto FL-421 E/Dunlawton Ave, turn right onto S Peninsula Dr, and continue for about 4 miles.

GPS Coordinates: 29.0807986° N, 80.9284404° W

Best Time to Visit: Fall and spring for milder weather

Pass/Permit/Fees: Adults: $6.95, children (3-11): $1.95

Did You Know? The lighthouse still operates as a private aid to navigation and its original first-order Fresnel lens is located in the museum.

Website: http://ponceinlet.org/

PUNTA GORDA

Fishermen's Village

Find your sense of charm and maritime history at Fishermen's Village, a waterfront destination in Punta Gorda, Florida. This unique complex features boutique shopping, waterfront dining, and lively entertainment. Located at the edge of Charlotte Harbor, it's the ideal spot for fishing, boat tours, and water sports. Stroll along the marina, enjoy the scenic views, and immerse yourself in the vibrant atmosphere of this charming coastal village. Whether you're shopping, dining, or enjoying the entertainment, there's something for everyone at Fishermen's Village.

Location: 1200 W Retta Esplanade #57a, Punta Gorda, FL 33950-5325

Closest City or Town: Punta Gorda, Florida

How to Get There: From I-75, take exit 164 for US-17 toward Punta Gorda, continue on US-17 S, turn right onto W Retta Esplanade.

GPS Coordinates: 26.9276923° N, 82.0637973° W

Best Time to Visit: Winter and spring for mild temperatures and fewer crowds

Pass/Permit/Fees: Free to explore; individual activity prices vary.

Did You Know? Fishermen's Village features a Military Heritage Museum housing extensive military artifacts from various U.S. wars.

Website: http://www.fishermensvillage.com/

SARASOTA

Mote Marine Laboratory & Aquarium

Dive into the underwater world at Mote Marine Laboratory & Aquarium, a premier research and education center in Sarasota, Florida. This cutting-edge facility offers interactive exhibits and up-close encounters with marine life, including sharks, manatees, and sea turtles. Located on Ken Thompson Parkway, Mote combines scientific research with public displays, providing a fascinating glimpse into marine conservation efforts. Enjoy touch pools, educational presentations, and the unique chance to see ongoing marine research in action.

Location: 1600 Ken Thompson Pkwy, Sarasota, FL 34236-1004

Closest City or Town: Sarasota, Florida

How to Get There: From US-41, take John Ringling Causeway west, turn right onto Ken Thompson Parkway.

GPS Coordinates: 27.3331533° N, 82.5773352° W

Best Time to Visit: Year-round; weekdays for quieter visits

Pass/Permit/Fees: General admission: Adults $24, children (3-12) $18

Did You Know? Mote Marine Laboratory houses the world's longest-running shark research program.

Website: http://mote.org/

Myakka River State Park

Embark on an adventure into the wild at Myakka River State Park, one of Florida's oldest and largest state parks. Located in Sarasota, this expansive park offers a range of outdoor activities, from hiking and wildlife photography to canoeing and airboat tours on the Myakka River. The park's lush landscapes are home to diverse wildlife, including alligators, herons, and rare Florida panthers. Explore the scenic trails, navigate the treetop canopy walk, or simply enjoy a picnic in this natural paradise.

Location: 13208 State Road 72, Sarasota, FL 34241-9546

Closest City or Town: Sarasota, Florida

How to Get There: From I-75, take exit 205 for FL-72/Clark Road east, and follow signs to Myakka River State Park.

GPS Coordinates: 27.2304832° N, 82.2691930° W

Best Time to Visit: Fall and winter for milder temperatures and active wildlife

Pass/Permit/Fees: Entrance fee: $6 per vehicle

Did You Know? Myakka River State Park's canopy walkway is the first public treetop trail in North America.

Website: http://www.floridastateparks.org/park/Myakka-River

St. Armands Circle

Discover the charm of St. Armands Circle, a vibrant shopping and dining destination located in Sarasota, Florida. This lushly landscaped circle offers a unique blend of upscale boutiques, gourmet restaurants, and lively entertainment, making it a haven for shoppers and foodies alike. Located on St. Armands Key, it's more than just a retail center; it's a cultural hub where you can stroll through art galleries, attend local events, and soak in the coastal atmosphere. A visit to St. Armands Circle promises an eclectic mix of leisure and luxury.

Location: 300 Madison Dr Suite 201, Sarasota, FL 34236-1300

Closest City or Town: Sarasota, Florida

How to Get There: From downtown Sarasota, head west on John Ringling Bridge/FL-789 W, then follow signs to St. Armands Circle.

GPS Coordinates: 27.3183915° N, 82.5772805° W

Best Time to Visit: Year-round, though evenings offer a lively atmosphere

Pass/Permit/Fees: Free to explore

Did You Know? St. Armands Circle was developed by circus magnate John Ringling, who envisioned it as a commercial hub.

Website: http://www.starmandscircleassoc.com/

The Ringling

Step into a world of art, culture, and history at The Ringling, an exceptional museum in Sarasota, Florida. Located on Bay Shore Road, this sprawling estate offers an unparalleled cultural experience with its extensive art collections, historic Ca' d'Zan mansion, and the fascinating Circus Museum. Visitors can explore European masterpieces, marvel at the grand architecture, and learn about the intriguing history of the circus. The Ringling provides a rich tapestry of experiences that cater to art lovers, history buffs, and those simply seeking a day of inspiration.

Location: 5401 Bay Shore Rd, Sarasota, FL 34243-2161

Closest City or Town: Sarasota, Florida

How to Get There: From downtown Sarasota, head north on US-41 N/Tamiami Trail, then turn left onto University Parkway and follow signs to The Ringling.

GPS Coordinates: 27.3825455° N, 82.5607250° W

Best Time to Visit: Year-round, with fewer crowds in early mornings

Pass/Permit/Fees: General admission starts at $25 for adults

Did You Know? The Ringling's Ca' d'Zan mansion was inspired by the palaces of Venice, reflecting John Ringling's love for the Venetian aesthetic.

Website: https://www.ringling.org/

SIESTA KEY

Siesta Beach

Find your sense of relaxation at Siesta Beach, renowned for its powdery white sand and clear blue waters. Located on Siesta Key, this beach is celebrated as one of the best in the U.S., perfect for sunbathing, swimming, and enjoying spectacular sunsets. Visitors can indulge in beach volleyball, paddleboarding, or simply unwind by the Gulf of Mexico. Siesta Beach offers a serene escape with top-notch amenities, making it an outstanding destination for a day of coastal bliss.

Location: 948 Beach Road, Siesta Key, FL 34242-2174

Closest City or Town: Siesta Key, Florida

How to Get There: From downtown Sarasota, take FL-780 W and follow signs for Siesta Key.

GPS Coordinates: 27.2657028° N, 82.5503109° W

Best Time to Visit: Spring and fall for perfect beach weather

Pass/Permit/Fees: Free to access, parking is available

Did You Know? The sand at Siesta Beach is 99% quartz, making it cool to the touch even on hot days.

Website: https://www.visitsarasota.com/article/siesta-key-no-1-beach-champion-destination

St. Augustine

Castillo de San Marcos National Monument

Explore the storied past at Castillo de San Marcos National Monument, the oldest masonry fort in the continental United States, located in St. Augustine, Florida. Built in the late 17th century, this formidable fortress offers a glimpse into colonial history through its well-preserved stone walls, cannons, and panoramic views of Matanzas Bay. Visitors can tour the fort, witness reenactments, and participate in educational programs that bring history to life. Whether you're a history buff or a casual traveler, Castillo de San Marcos is a captivating journey back in time.

Location: 1 S Castillo Dr, St. Augustine, FL 32084-3252

Closest City or Town: St. Augustine, Florida

How to Get There: From downtown St. Augustine, head north on Avenida Menendez, then turn right onto Castillo Drive.

GPS Coordinates: 29.8978055° N, 81.3132262° W

Best Time to Visit: Year-round, with cooler weather in fall and winter

Pass/Permit/Fees: $15 per adult; children under 15 are free

Did You Know? Castillo de San Marcos has never been taken in battle, thanks to its resilient coquina stone walls.

Website: http://www.nps.gov/casa

Lightner Museum

Delve into the elegance of the past at Lightner Museum, located in St. Augustine, Florida. Housed in the historic Alcazar Hotel, this museum features a dazzling array of Gilded Age art and antiques, including Victorian glass, fine paintings, and period costumes. Located on King Street, the Lightner offers a rich cultural experience amid its opulent architecture and serene gardens. Visitors can explore the meticulously curated exhibits, enjoy live music performances, and dine in the historic setting of the museum's cafe. It's a must-visit for art and history enthusiasts.

Location: 75 King St, St. Augustine, FL 32084-4386

Closest City or Town: St. Augustine, Florida

How to Get There: From downtown St. Augustine, head west on King Street and the museum will be on your left.

GPS Coordinates: 29.8908690° N, 81.3137957° W

Best Time to Visit: Year-round, with fewer crowds in the early morning

Pass/Permit/Fees: General admission is $15 for adults

Did You Know? The Lightner Museum occupies the former Alcazar Hotel, built by railroad magnate Henry Flagler in 1888.

Website: http://www.lightnermuseum.org/

Old Jail Museum

Find your sense of intrigue at the Old Jail Museum, a historic gem situated in St. Augustine, Florida. This preserved structure, reminiscent of an era gone by, offers visitors a deep dive into the lives of prisoners and sheriffs from the late 19th and early 20th centuries. Located on San Marco Avenue, the museum provides guided tours featuring live reenactments and fascinating stories, painting a vivid picture of life within its formidable walls. The unique architecture, complete with iron bars and a gallows, adds an authentic touch to this memorable experience, ensuring you leave with both chills and insights.

Location: 167 San Marco Ave, St. Augustine, FL 32084-3269

Closest City or Town: St. Augustine, Florida

How to Get There: From I-95, take exit 318 to SR-16 East. Continue on SR-16 East and turn right onto San Marco Avenue.

GPS Coordinates: 29.9080130° N, 81.3186120° W

Best Time to Visit: Spring and fall for milder weather

Pass/Permit/Fees: General admission: $15.99 for adults, $9.99 for children

Did You Know? The Old Jail is listed on the National Register of Historic Places and once housed some of the region's most notorious criminals.

Website: https://www.visitstaugustine.com/thing-to-do/old-jail

St. Augustine Alligator Farm Zoological Park

Find your sense of wild adventure at the St. Augustine Alligator Farm Zoological Park, where the realm of reptiles comes to life. Located on Anastasia Boulevard, this zoological park is home to every living species of crocodilian, along with exotic birds, mammals, and reptiles from around the globe. Dive into exciting experiences such as zip-lining over alligator habitats, feeding shows, and interactive exhibits. Unique features include Maximo, a 15-foot saltwater crocodile, and Albino Alligators. The park's blend of entertainment and education makes it a must-see for animal enthusiasts and thrill-seekers alike.

Location: 999 Anastasia Blvd, St. Augustine, FL 32080-4619

Closest City or Town: St. Augustine, Florida

How to Get There: Head east on FL-312 from US-1, turn left onto Anastasia Blvd.

GPS Coordinates: 29.8818461° N, 81.2885721° W

Best Time to Visit: Spring and early summer for warm weather and active animals

Pass/Permit/Fees: General admission: $27.99 for adults, $16.99 for children

Did You Know? The Alligator Farm is the world's only facility with every species of crocodilian.

Website: http://www.alligatorfarm.com/

St. Augustine Beach

Soak up the sun at St. Augustine Beach, a picturesque coastal gem along Florida's Atlantic coastline. Located on 8th Street, this beach offers stunning vistas of white sand and shimmering blue waves, ideal for swimming, surfing, and sunbathing. This family-friendly destination also features a pier for fishing, volleyball courts, and picnic areas. The welcoming atmosphere and easy access make it perfect for a leisurely beach day. Whether you're building sandcastles or simply relaxing under the sun, St. Augustine Beach promises a quintessential Florida beach experience.

Location: 1 8th St, St. Augustine, FL 32080

Closest City or Town: St. Augustine, Florida

How to Get There: From US-1, head east on FL-312, then continue on A1A South.

GPS Coordinates: 29.8505459° N, 81.2646917° W

Best Time to Visit: Summer months for optimal beach weather

Pass/Permit/Fees: Free to access; parking fees may apply

Did You Know? St. Augustine Beach is also a great spot for sea turtle nesting, typically from May to October.

Website: https://www.staugbch.com/

St. Augustine Lighthouse & Maritime Museum, Inc

Uncover maritime history at the St. Augustine Lighthouse & Maritime Museum, Inc, a beacon of heritage located on Red Cox Drive. This historic lighthouse offers panoramic views of the nation's oldest city and its pristine coastline. Enjoy climbing the 219 steps to the top, exploring exhibits on shipwrecks and maritime archaeology, and participating in behind-the-scenes tours. The museum also offers ghost tours for those with a taste for the supernatural. Unique to this landmark are the working conservation labs, where ongoing efforts preserve the region's nautical artifacts.

Location: 100 Red Cox Dr, St. Augustine, FL 32080-5443

Closest City or Town: St. Augustine, Florida

How to Get There: From downtown St. Augustine, take the Bridge of Lions to Anastasia Blvd, then turn left onto Red Cox Drive.

GPS Coordinates: 29.8853844° N, 81.2882812° W

Best Time to Visit: Spring and fall for pleasant weather and fewer crowds

Pass/Permit/Fees: General admission: $12.95 for adults, $10.95 for seniors and children

Did You Know? The lighthouse was built in 1874 and still serves as an active aid to navigation today.

Website: http://staugustinelighthouse.org/

St. Augustine Pirate & Treasure Museum

Discover tales of high seas and buried gold at the St. Augustine Pirate & Treasure Museum, an engaging attraction at South Castillo Drive. This interactive museum takes you through the Golden Age of Piracy with authentic artifacts, hands-on exhibits, and immersive displays. Located near the historic Castillo de San Marcos, the museum lets you experience the life of a pirate, view relics of infamous figures like Blackbeard, and even try your hand at a treasure hunt. Unique features include one of only three surviving Jolly Roger flags.

Location: 12 S Castillo Dr, St. Augustine, FL 32084-3650

Closest City or Town: St. Augustine, Florida

How to Get There: From US-1, head east on King Street, then turn left onto South Castillo Drive.

GPS Coordinates: 29.8970170° N, 81.3129660° W

Best Time to Visit: Year-round, with fewer crowds in the mornings

Pass/Permit/Fees: General admission: $13.99 for adults, $6.99 for children

Did You Know? The museum boasts the world's only known pirate treasure chest.

Website: https://www.facebook.com/ThePirateMuseum/

St. Augustine Wild Reserve

Find your sense of adventure and marvel at the magnificent creatures of the wild at St. Augustine Wild Reserve. Located in St. Augustine, Florida, this sanctuary offers an intimate glimpse into the world of exotic animals, including lions, tigers, bears, and wolves. Engage in guided tours showcasing the reserve's commitment to conservation and education, while learning fascinating stories about the animals and their habitats. This unique experience promises unforgettable encounters with some of nature's most majestic inhabitants.

Location: 5190 Farm Creek Rd, St. Augustine, FL 32092-0651

Closest City or Town: St. Augustine, Florida

How to Get There: From I-95, take exit 323 to International Golf Parkway; head west, then turn left onto US-16; drive for approximately 3 miles and turn right onto CR-13A to reach Farm Creek Rd.

GPS Coordinates: 29.9511070° N, 81.5126340° W

Best Time to Visit: Spring and fall for mild weather and active animals

Pass/Permit/Fees: Entrance fees apply; please check the website for details

Did You Know? The reserve was established to provide a safe haven for unwanted exotic animals, many of which have been rescued from less favorable conditions.

Website: https://www.sawildreserve.org/

St. George Street

Find your sense of history and culture as you stroll down St. George Street, a charming pedestrian thoroughfare in the heart of St. Augustine, Florida. This historic avenue offers a journey through time with its beautifully preserved architecture, eclectic shops, and vibrant eateries. Wander through historic sites, stop by local markets, and savor the blend of old-world charm and modern vibrancy. A walk down St. George Street encapsulates the rich heritage and enduring spirit of one of America's oldest cities.

Location: St. George St, St. Augustine, FL 32084

Closest City or Town: St. Augustine, Florida

How to Get There: From US-1 S, turn left onto W Castillo Dr, then turn right onto Cordova St, and continue to Castillo Drive; St. George Street is directly accessible by foot.

GPS Coordinates: 29.8927093° N, 81.3128181° W

Best Time to Visit: Spring and fall for pleasant weather and fewer crowds

Pass/Permit/Fees: Free to explore

Did You Know? St. George Street is lined with centuries-old buildings, including the oldest wooden schoolhouse in the United States.

Website: http://www.visitflorida.com/en-us/culture/articles/11/1853-st-george-street-walkable-journey-into-st-augustine-history-culture.html

ST. PETE BEACH

St. Pete Beach

Soak up the sun and endless fun at St. Pete Beach, a picturesque coastal retreat located on Florida's Gulf Coast. Known for its powdery white sand and clear blue waters, this beach is an ideal spot for swimming, sunbathing, and a variety of water sports. Enjoy a leisurely day exploring local shops, dining at beachfront restaurants, and watching the stunning sunsets over the Gulf of Mexico. St. Pete Beach offers a perfect blend of relaxation and adventure.

Location: Gulf Blvd, St. Pete Beach, FL 33706

Closest City or Town: St. Pete Beach, Florida

How to Get There: From I-275, take exit 17 onto FL-682 W/54th Ave S; continue on 54th Ave S, follow signs to Gulf Blvd.

GPS Coordinates: 27.7216694° N, 82.7404587° W

Best Time to Visit: Spring and fall for ideal beach weather

Pass/Permit/Fees: Free; parking fees vary by location

Did You Know? St. Pete Beach is home to the iconic pink Don CeSar Hotel, a historic landmark known as the Pink Palace.

Website: https://www.visitstpeteclearwater.com/

St. Petersburg

Chihuly Collection

Find your sense of wonder and artistic inspiration at the Chihuly Collection, a stunning display of glass art located in St. Petersburg, Florida. Renowned artist Dale Chihuly's vibrant and dynamic works are showcased in an intimate setting, offering a unique opportunity to experience his creative brilliance up close. Located on Central Avenue, visitors can admire an array of mesmerizing glass sculptures through expertly designed installations that highlight their intricate beauty and imaginative forms.

Location: 720 Central Ave, St. Petersburg, FL 33701-3643

Closest City or Town: St. Petersburg, Florida

How to Get There: From I-275, take exit 23A to merge onto I-375 E; continue on I-375 E, turn right onto 8th St N, then turn left onto Central Ave.

GPS Coordinates: 27.7710260° N, 82.6440401° W

Best Time to Visit: Year-round; weekdays for a quieter experience

Pass/Permit/Fees: General admission: $20 for adults

Did You Know? The Chihuly Collection is the only permanent collection of Dale Chihuly's work that was designed by the artist himself.

Website: https://moreanartscenter.org/chihuly-collection-location/

Sunken Gardens

Immerse yourself in a lush tropical oasis at Sunken Gardens, a botanical paradise located in St. Petersburg, Florida. This century-old garden, home to more than 50,000 plants and flowers, offers visitors a tranquil escape with winding paths, cascading waterfalls, and serene ponds. Located on 4th Street North, the garden provides the perfect setting for leisurely strolls and peaceful reflection, while learning about diverse plant species from around the world.

Location: 1825 4th St N, St. Petersburg, FL 33704-4397

Closest City or Town: St. Petersburg, Florida

How to Get There: From I-275, take exit 24 for 22nd Ave N, head east, then turn right onto 4th St N.

GPS Coordinates: 27.7897718° N, 82.6378269° W

Best Time to Visit: Spring and fall for mild weather and vibrant blooms

Pass/Permit/Fees: General admission: $10 for adults, $4 for children (ages 2-11)

Did You Know? Sunken Gardens is one of the oldest family-owned attractions in Florida, having opened in 1935.

Website:
http://www.stpete.org/attractions/sunken_gardens/index.php

Sunshine Skyway Bridge

Bask in the splendor of the Sunshine Skyway Bridge, the crown jewel of Tampa Bay. This iconic bridge, stretching gracefully over the sparkling waters, offers breathtaking panoramic views that make it a must-drive for any scenic enthusiast. Located in St. Petersburg, this engineering marvel connects the cities of Tampa and Bradenton, becoming a glittering beacon in Florida's coastal landscape. Enjoy a picturesque drive, marvel at the sweeping aesthetics, or stop by the fishing piers for a tranquil escape. This destination invites you to find your sense of adventure and marvel at human and natural grandeur.

Location: 7508 7534 Sunshine Skyway Lane S, St. Petersburg, FL 33711

Closest City or Town: St. Petersburg, Florida

How to Get There: From I-275, take Exit 16 for Skyway Ln S towards Sunshine Skyway. The bridge entrance will be clearly marked.

GPS Coordinates: 27.6982667° N, 82.6782356° W

Best Time to Visit: Early morning or late afternoon for the best views.

Pass/Permit/Fees: Toll fees apply; check the website for current rates.

Did You Know? The Sunshine Skyway Bridge is one of the longest cable-stayed concrete bridges in the world.

Website: https://www.facebook.com/sunshineskyway.bridge/

The Dali Museum

Step into the surreal world of Salvador Dali at The Dali Museum in St. Petersburg. This architectural masterpiece houses the largest collection of Dali's works outside Europe and takes you on a journey through his eccentric artistic vision. Located on the downtown waterfront, the museum combines inventive exhibits with stunning views of Tampa Bay. Admire the detailed craftsmanship of Dali's paintings, explore avant-garde installations, or participate in engaging workshops. Immerse yourself in the whimsy and creativity, celebrating one of modern art's most fascinating figures.

Location: One Dali Blvd, St. Petersburg, FL 33701-4901

Closest City or Town: St. Petersburg, Florida

How to Get There: From I-275, take Exit 22 for I-175 E toward Tropicana Field, then follow signs to Dali Blvd.

GPS Coordinates: 27.7657203° N, 82.6346808° W

Best Time to Visit: Weekdays, early morning to mid-afternoon for smaller crowds.

Pass/Permit/Fees: General admission: $25 for adults, $18 for students with identification.

Did You Know? The "Glass Enigma" dome structure at the museum consists of more than 1,000 triangular pieces of glass.

Website: http://thedali.org/

SURFSIDE

Collins Avenue

Discover vibrant luxury on Collins Avenue, Miami Beach's bustling boulevard lined with top-tier hotels, boutiques, and dazzling nightlife. Located in Surfside, this iconic thoroughfare hosts a glamorous mix of high-end shopping and cultural landmarks. Stroll along the palm-lined sidewalks, admire the striking Art Deco architecture, or dine at world-class restaurants. Collins Avenue is where fashion meets fun, making it a key stop for anyone wanting to experience Miami's glitz and charm.

Location: 9418 Collins Ave, Surfside, FL 33154

Closest City or Town: Surfside, Florida

How to Get There: From I-95, take Exit 10A for NW 125th St, continue east onto 125th St/North Shore Dr, then merge onto FL-A1A S toward Collins Ave.

GPS Coordinates: 25.8839071° N, 80.1227067° W

Best Time to Visit: Evenings for vibrant nightlife.

Pass/Permit/Fees: Free to explore; store and restaurant prices vary.

Did You Know? Collins Avenue is named after John Stiles Collins, a Quaker farmer who built the first wooden bridge connecting Miami to Miami Beach in 1913.

Website: https://www.miamiandbeaches.com/l/shopping/collins-avenue-ocean-drive-shopping-district/1235

TAMPA

Busch Gardens

Unleash your wild side at Busch Gardens, a thrilling theme park and zoo located in Tampa, Florida. This African-themed adventure land boasts exhilarating rides like SheiKra, a floorless dive coaster, and animal encounters with species from around the world. Covering 335 acres, it offers activities from high-adrenaline roller coasters to serene botanical gardens. Live shows and events provide constant entertainment, while the Serengeti Safari offers an unforgettable wildlife experience. Busch Gardens fuses the thrill of a theme park with the wonder of a world-class zoo.

Location: 10165 McKinley Dr, Tampa, FL 33612

Closest City or Town: Tampa, Florida

How to Get There: From I-275, take Exit 51 for Fowler Ave, head east, and follow signs to Busch Gardens.

GPS Coordinates: 28.0370660° N, 82.4194607° W

Best Time to Visit: Weekdays during school months for fewer crowds.

Pass/Permit/Fees: Admission starts at $89.99 for adults; various passes are available.

Did You Know? Busch Gardens Tampa Bay is home to more than 200 species of animals and was one of the first U.S. parks to implement a free-roaming animal habitat.

Website: http://buschgardens.com/tampa

The Florida Aquarium

Dive into the depths of aquatic wonder at The Florida Aquarium, a captivating destination nestled along Tampa's Channelside Drive. This expansive marine paradise offers an up-close look at Gulf of Mexico wildlife, including colorful tropical fish, inquisitive stingrays, and mysterious sharks. Spanning 250,000 square feet, the aquarium presents a journey through Florida's watery ecosystems, from wetlands to coral reefs. Interactive touch tanks, the stunning Coral

Reef tunnel, and unique wildlife encounters make it an educational yet thrilling family adventure.

Location: 701 Channelside Dr, Tampa, FL 33602-5600

Closest City or Town: Tampa, Florida

How to Get There: From I-275, take Exit 44 for Downtown East and follow signs to Channelside Drive.

GPS Coordinates: 27.9439720° N, 82.4448747° W

Best Time to Visit: Weekdays and early mornings to avoid the crowd.

Pass/Permit/Fees: General admission: $29.95 for adults; discounts for children and seniors.

Did You Know? The Florida Aquarium is home to one of the most prestigious coral conservation programs in the country.

Website: http://www.flaquarium.org/

Ybor City

Find your sense of cultural exploration in Ybor City, a vibrant historic district northeast of Downtown Tampa. Founded in the 1880s by Cuban cigar manufacturers, this neighborhood is rich with cultural heritage and bustling nightlife. Stroll along its picturesque streets, dine at authentic Cuban restaurants, and immerse yourself in the unique historic streetcar experience. Visit the Ybor City Museum to learn about its storied past and explore eclectic shops, lively bars, and charming cafes.

Location: Northeast of the Downtown Tampa on I-4 at Exit 1, Tampa, FL 33618

Closest City or Town: Tampa, Florida

How to Get There: From I-4, take Exit 1 to 21st Street and follow the signs to Ybor City.

GPS Coordinates: 27.9505750° N, 82.4571776° W

Best Time to Visit: Fall and winter for cooler temperatures and festive events

Pass/Permit/Fees: Free to explore; individual activity prices vary

Did You Know? Ybor City is known as the Cigar Capital of the World due to its rich history in cigar manufacturing.

Website: http://ybor.org/

ZooTampa At Lowry Park

Embark on a wild adventure at ZooTampa At Lowry Park, where nature meets excitement in Tampa, Florida. This renowned zoo offers over 1,300 animals across lush, tropical landscapes. Witness majestic manatees, playful primates, and rare wildlife from around the world. The zoo's engaging exhibits, such as the Florida Wilds and Wallaroo Station, provide interactive learning experiences for all ages. Nestled along the Hillsborough River, ZooTampa also hosts seasonal events and animal encounters that make for unforgettable family outings.

Location: 1101 W Sligh Ave, Tampa, FL 33604-5958

Closest City or Town: Tampa, Florida

How to Get There: From I-275, take exit 48 for Sligh Avenue, and follow signs to the zoo.

GPS Coordinates: 28.0138361° N, 82.4699672° W

Best Time to Visit: Spring and fall for pleasant weather and active animals

Pass/Permit/Fees: General admission: Adults $39.95, children (3-11) $29.95

Did You Know? ZooTampa is one of the leading zoos in the country for manatee rehabilitation.

Website: http://www.zootampa.org/

TIERRA VERDE

Fort De Soto Park

Discover outdoor paradise at Fort De Soto Park, a pristine coastal haven located in Tierra Verde, Florida. Spanning 1,136 acres across five interconnected islands, this park is a dream for nature lovers and history buffs alike. Explore miles of trails, enjoy pristine beaches, and tour the historic fort that dates back to the Spanish-American War. Offering activities like kayaking, fishing, and bird-watching, Fort De Soto is also home to a year-round camping area, making it ideal for both day trips and overnight adventures.

Location: 3500 Pinellas Bayway South, Tierra Verde, FL 33715-2529

Closest City or Town: Tierra Verde, Florida

How to Get There: From I-275, take Exit 17 for Pinellas Bayway S and follow signs to the park entrance.

GPS Coordinates: 27.6338498° N, 82.7186092° W

Best Time to Visit: Year-round, though spring and fall offer milder weather

Pass/Permit/Fees: $5 per vehicle entrance fee

Did You Know? Fort De Soto Park's North Beach was named America's Best Beach by TripAdvisor in 2008.

Website: http://www.pinellascounty.org/park/05_Ft_DeSoto.htm

WEST PALM BEACH

McCarthy's Wildlife Sanctuary

Find your sense of wonder at McCarthy's Wildlife Sanctuary in West Palm Beach, Florida. This unique sanctuary is home to over 200 animals, including big cats, exotic birds, and reptiles. Offering guided tours, McCarthy's provides a personal and educational experience as visitors learn about wildlife conservation and get up-close with the animals. Located in a lush, natural setting, the sanctuary is dedicated to rescuing and rehabilitating distressed animals while educating the public about wildlife preservation.

Location: 12943 61st St N, West Palm Beach, FL 33412-2017

Closest City or Town: West Palm Beach, Florida

How to Get There: From I-95, take Exit 79 for PGA Boulevard and head west. Turn right onto Seminole Pratt Whitney Road, then left onto 61st Street North.

GPS Coordinates: 26.7675498° N, 80.2458135° W

Best Time to Visit: Year-round, but mornings offer cooler temperatures and active animals

Pass/Permit/Fees: General admission: $35 per person (tour reservations required)

Did You Know? McCarthy's Wildlife Sanctuary has been rescuing animals and providing sanctuary for over 30 years.

Website: http://www.mccarthyswildlife.com/

Winter Haven

Legoland Florida Resort

Find your sense of play and imagination at Legoland Florida Resort, a whimsical wonderland in Winter Haven, Florida. Perfect for families with children ages 2-12, this theme park features over 50 rides, shows, and interactive attractions inspired by the beloved Lego bricks. Located on the shores of Lake Eloise, the resort also includes a water park and the immersive Lego Ninjago World. Highlights include Miniland USA, with Lego replicas of iconic cities, and fun-filled experiences like building and racing your own Lego car.

Location: 1 Legoland Way, Winter Haven, FL 33884-4139

Closest City or Town: Winter Haven, Florida

How to Get There: From I-4, take Exit 55 for US-27 South, continue on US-27 South, and follow signs to Legoland Florida Resort.

GPS Coordinates: 27.9898932° N, 81.6914153° W

Best Time to Visit: Spring and fall for mild weather and fewer crowds

Pass/Permit/Fees: General admission varies; check website for seasonal rates

Did You Know? Legoland Florida Resort is built on the site of the former Cypress Gardens, a historic Florida attraction.

Website: http://legoland.com/florida

MAP

We have devised an interactive map that includes all destinations described in the book.

Upon scanning a provided QR code, a link will be sent to your email, allowing you access to this unique digital feature.

This map is both detailed and user-friendly, marking every location described within the pages of the book. It provides accurate addresses and GPS coordinates for each location, coupled with direct links to the websites of these stunning destinations.

Once you receive your email link and access the interactive map, you'll have an immediate and comprehensive overview of each site's location. This invaluable tool simplifies trip planning and navigation, making it a crucial asset for both first-time visitors and seasoned explorers of Washington.

Scan the following QR or type in the provided link to receive it:

https://jo.my/floridanbucketlistbonus

You will receive an email with links to access the Interactive Map. If you do not see our email, please look for it in spam or another section of your inbox.

In case you have any problems, you can write us at
TravelBucketList@becrepress.com

Made in the USA
Monee, IL
09 December 2024

73068611R00066